THE GREAT MARGARITA BOOK

AL LUCERO

WITH JOHN HARRISSON

SECOND EDITION

BARNES & NOBLE

NEW YORK

Cover design by Gary Bernal
Text design by Chris Hall (based on a design
by Gary Bernal)

Photographs on pages 34, 37, 43–7, 52–3, 61, 63–7,
69, 70–1, 77–8, 80–2, 90, 99, 100–05, 107–18, and
121–9 by Lois Ellen Frank. All other photographs
by Scott Vlaun.

Library of Congress Cataloging-in-Publication data
on file with publisher.

This edition published exclusively for Barnes &
Noble, Inc., by Ten Speed Press

ISBN 0-7607-7853-1

Printed in Hong Kong

1 2 3 4 6 7 8 9 10 — 08 07 06

CONTENTS

FOREWORD
1

INTRODUCTION
2

CHAPTER ONE
Tequila:
The Soul of a Real Margarita
5

CHAPTER TWO
Other Essentials for a Great Margarita
13

CHAPTER THREE
The Noble Origins of the Margarita
19

CHAPTER FOUR
Recipes for Real Margaritas
29

CHAPTER FIVE
More Great Tequila Drinks
130

CHAPTER SIX
Maria's New Mexican Kitchen:
Food to Serve with Margaritas
137

INDEX
144

FOREWORD

There was a time when a state of mind could be defined or cured by a good martini. It was a benchmark for a good time, a good lunch, a good date, a great place. The Great American Drink.

No more. Now, more often than not, in more places than most, that American measuring stick has given way to the new king: the Margarita. I don't know where or when or even how this started. I just know it's here. So now we hear about restaurants or bars defined by how great their margaritas are.

What constitutes a truly great margarita is not that easy to define. It is at once elusive and unforgiving. I once had a margarita in Westport, Connecticut, and threw up an hour later. I've had margaritas that were watered down, over-sweetened, too sour, and some strange color. (Can there be a good strawberry margarita?) One thing is certain. When you have a real margarita, you know it.

When people have asked of a place to eat in Santa Fe, I find myself referring them to Maria's. Is it fancy? No. Is it chic? No. Is the food good? Yes. But the margaritas—they are the best. When you read this book, you'll know why. Like anything of quality, it takes love and care—a degree of passion to execute it, love to start it, commitment to that love to sustain it. Maria's is a history and a definition. I am glad it's there. I'm glad I've tasted their margaritas, and I hope not too many people find out about it.

Robert Redford

Robert Redford

INTRODUCTION

I can remember first seeing the Maria's sign out front of the adobe-style building when I was about fourteen or fifteen years old, back in the early fifties. I was born and raised in Santa Fe, New Mexico, and back then a new restaurant was big news. The only others I can remember are the Pink Adobe, the Pantry, El Gancho on the old Las Vegas Highway (now Old Pecos Trail), and a truck stop out on old Highway 85 (Cerrillos Road). Of course there was the La Fonda Hotel (a Santa Fe landmark), and I knew there was a "ritzy" restaurant inside, but it was only for adults and tourists with lots of money.

The state had just moved the old New Mexico state penitentiary south of town (having razed the old pen, which was located catty-corner to Maria's). Little did I imagine that the original owners of Maria's would be buying the used brick from the demolition of the pen to decorate the inside of a restaurant that, thirty years later, I would own.

Maria's is not just a historic Santa Fe landmark; it almost qualifies as a museum. The beer cooler is a converted icebox dating back to the 1880s that was shipped in from its perch in the old gold rush town of Dawson in northern New Mexico. (My dad was a six-gun-toting deputy U.S. marshal in the area of Dawson at the turn of the century, so he could have easily had a couple of beers from that very icebox while it was still in its original spot.) The hand-carved and painted beams in the east room come from the old Public Service Company building in downtown Santa Fe. Much of the furniture throughout the restaurant is from the pre–World War II La Fonda Hotel. And the famous Santa Fe artist Alfred Morang painted wall frescoes in the cantina in exchange for food and drink. (We had these priceless paintings restored by local restoration experts who relished the job because of their admiration for Morang. Now the work of dozens of other Santa Fe artists hangs on the walls of Maria's as well.)

The Maria's tradition began in 1950 when Maria Lopez and her husband, Gilbert, started a take-out kitchen on the very same spot, in the very same building where Maria's exists today. As business boomed for the young Lopez couple, they slowly expanded, adding two booths and a patio.

Over the years, Maria's had its ups and downs. My wife, Laurie, and I are the fifth owners of Maria's. After moving back to Santa Fe following my career as a television executive (which took us all over the country), Laurie and I, like a lot of other couples, used to dine out a lot. We would critique each restaurant we visited and tell each other how we could have made it better. Relying on this great store of knowledge, we bought Maria's on December 1, 1985. We had history on our side: I am an umpteenth-generation descendant of one of the old Spanish conquistadors who captained an army that occupied Santa Fe in the seventeenth century—so my family has been cooking and eating New Mexican food for centuries.

Before we moved back to Santa Fe, we had been looking forward to enjoying the wonderful New Mexican cooking at local restaurants. Unfortunately, once we got there we were disappointed. Some things had changed since I was a kid. Soupy beans and posole were being served on the plate with no broth. Tacos were being filled with roast beef and potatoes. Tortillas were all machine made. Margaritas were being poured out of slush-type machines. I had been making margaritas in a blender, using sweetened, frozen lime juice as far back as the 1960s. I can remember adding sugar to give the slush some flavor. Shortly after buying Maria's, I discovered that making margaritas with lime or lemon juice, triple sec, and tequila shaken with ice brought out the flavors of the ingredients. That was when I started experimenting with various tequilas. When we bought Maria's, we decided we were going to do things right. And we did. We served beans and posole in a bowl with broth, we made our tortillas by hand, and we introduced properly served fajitas to Santa Fe—which of course had to be accompanied by margaritas!

Having researched other aspects of our restaurant to make sure that it was as authentic as possible, we were determined to make the best margarita anywhere in the world! We studied up on tequila in Mexico and emphasized the quality and flavor of 100 percent agave tequila, mixing it with freshly squeezed lemon or lime juice and naturally flavored triple sec, rather than manufactured sugar-sweetened drink mixes. We were amazed what a difference it made to use only the best-quality ingredients.

Our attention to detail and our determination to make the best and purest margaritas possible have paid off. The *New York Times* called Maria's margaritas the "best in town." The *Washington Post* said they are "world class." *Southern Arts* described Maria's as "Margaritaville" and named our margaritas as one of the 101 reasons to visit Santa Fe. The *Seattle*

Times described us as "the mother lode of American margaritas." From *Better Homes and Gardens* to *Playboy,* newspapers and magazines nationwide, as well as almost every state and local publication, have given our margaritas rave reviews.

Most Americans are used to drinking poor or mediocre tequila, whether straight or in a margarita. The purpose of this book is to share the knowledge of how to recognize and appreciate a good tequila, and how to make the purest, most delightful cocktail on earth: a great margarita!

¡Salud!

Al Lucero

CHAPTER ONE

TEQUILA
The Soul of a
Real Margarita

You want a great margarita, right? Then it makes sense that you should use only the best ingredients to make it, especially when it comes to tequila. At Maria's in Santa Fe, we call our great margaritas "real margaritas" because we use only real ingredients: real tequila, real triple sec, and real lemon or lime juice. However, just because a bottle has the word "tequila" on its label does not automatically mean that it contains real tequila. So it's important to learn the basic facts about tequila.

Tequila is an 80-proof liquor (40 percent alcohol by volume) that is made only in Mexico. It is double distilled from the sugary juices extracted from the cooked *piña*, or heart, of the blue agave plant (botanically named *Agave tequilana Weber*, blue variety). Although there are 360 varieties of agave, the blue agave is the only one from which tequila can be made.

By the early 1990s, tequila had become the tenth-best-selling spirit in the United States (vodka is the market leader). The United States not only imports more tequila than any other country in the world, but it also consumes more tequila than Mexico. Tequila is also the fastest-growing spirit in terms of sales, largely because of the ever-increasing popularity of margaritas.

The Mexican government maintains strict control over the production of tequila and imposes exacting regulations on its distillers, the most important of which mandates that all tequila must be distilled twice and must contain at least 51 percent blue agave sugar. Any product with less than 51 percent blue agave sugar cannot, by the Mexican government's standards, be considered tequila. So from now on we'll call tequila with 51 percent or more agave sugar "real" tequila and that with less than 51 percent agave sugar "unreal."

The agave sugars used in making tequila can best be described by comparing the manufacturing of tequila to the making of maple syrup. If one were to take the sap of a maple tree and mix it with corn syrup, it would not be pure maple syrup; it would be syrup with natural maple flavoring. Obviously, the higher the percentage of pure maple sap (sugar) used to make the syrup, the better the maple flavor that would result. The same chemistry applies to tequila. The higher the percentage of agave sugar used to make the tequila, the better the quality of the tequila. If the tequila is made with less than 100 percent agave sugar (known as a "mixto"), cane sugar dissolved in distilled water is added.

In addition to regulating the percentage of agave sugar, the Mexican government also requires that the agave plants used to make real tequila can only be grown in one of five Mexican states: Jalisco, Michoacán, Nayarit, Tamaulipas, or Guanajuato. Like fine Burgundy wines grown in different microclimates of adjacent valleys and mountainsides, there is a distinctive difference in flavor between tequilas (such as El Tesoro and Patrón) grown in the highlands of Jalisco around Arandas, and those (like José Cuervo) grown in the foothills near the village of Tequila, which is still the center of the tequila industry.

After the required 51 percent blue agave sugar, the remaining 49 percent (or less) of the liquid in tequila is generally water with cane sugar (usually Mexican grown), which is added to the blue agave sugar during fermentation. Some tequilas contain much more than the required 51 percent blue agave; however, only those tequilas that are 100 percent blue agave are required to list this percentage on the label. It is also required that each bottle of tequila (whether bottled in Mexico or elsewhere) carry the distiller's NOM (*Norma Oficial Mexicana*, or "official Mexican standard") number. This four-digit number is issued only to tequila distillers who can consistently pass government inspections and comply with the required regulations for the production of tequila. If a bottle of tequila does not have the distiller's NOM number on the label, it is not real tequila, even if the label says "Made in Mexico."

To appreciate premium tequila fully, it is important to understand that there are significant differences between premium tequila that merely complies with the Mexican government's minimum requirement of 51 percent blue agave and the best-quality superpremium tequila distilled from 100 percent blue agave juice (known as *miel* in Mexico) with nothing else added.

All 100 percent blue agave tequilas must be bottled in Mexico and can only be exported in their original bottles. On the other hand, other tequilas can be and usually are exported in railroad tank cars or tanker trucks and then bottled at plants in various cities, usually in the United States.

Both premium and superpremium tequilas come in several different grades. Here is where it gets interesting: different grades of tequila result in different kinds of margaritas. The different types of tequila are categorized as *plata* or *blanco* ("silver" or "white" tequila); gold, also called *joven abocado* ("young and smoothed"); *reposado* ("rested," or aged for a brief time); *añejo* ("aged"); and *muy añejo* ("very aged").

Plata is freshly fermented and double-distilled tequila, which is usually bottled or shipped immediately after distillation. Premium plata tequila, like all other premium tequilas, is bottled in Mexico and shipped in the bottle. Plata is the most commonly produced of all tequilas. I personally enjoy premium plata tequila more than any other, whether for sipping or for my favorite cocktail, a great margarita.

Gold (or joven abocado) tequila (are you ready to have your lifelong Jimmy Buffett image of tequila destroyed?) is generally freshly distilled plata with caramel food coloring added to darken its appearance and give it an attractive golden hue. The Spanish word for gold, *oro*, actually is very seldom used in describing tequila; rather, añejo or muy añejo is used. Aged tequilas may be gold in color also, but the color is the result of the process of aging in oak barrels (the longer it's aged in oak, the darker the color).

Reposado tequila is carefully aged in oak barrels for a minimum of two months and for no longer than one year. The color of the tequila will take on a little of the oaken tint from the wooden barrel, but sometimes the difference between plata tequila and reposado is almost indistinguishable. The "resting" process enhances the flavor of reposado and may make the tequila a bit more mellow, but it does not really affect the flavor of a margarita. Most reposado tequilas are superpremium 100 percent agave tequilas.

Añejo tequila has been aged in oak barrels for a minimum of one year, a process that must be certified by the Mexican government. The color of añejo tequila varies, but most often it is a soft golden hue, not the deep gold of artificially colored "gold" tequilas. Almost all añejo and muy añejo tequilas are superpremium tequilas.

Muy añejo tequila is aged in oak barrels for more than two years and, as with añejo tequila, the aging process must be certified by the Mexican government. The color of muy añejo tequila is naturally darker than the añejo because it has been exposed to the oak wood longer; its coloring comes from the oak. Like a fine cognac, muy añejo is wonderful for sipping, and it also creates a distinctive taste treat when used in a margarita.

Unlike whisky, tequila does not age well over long periods of time. As a matter of fact, tequila will reach its peak in oak in two to four years. If left on oak for five or six years, tequila is almost always "turned" (spoiled)—

much like bottled wine that has not been properly stored. However, once bottled, tequila will keep as well as most other distilled spirits; and like other spirits, it finishes aging once it's removed from the oak barrels.

Two other Mexican liquors, mezcal and pulque, are sometimes confused with tequila. The one that sometimes has a worm in the bottle is mezcal (the worm inside a mezcal bottle is actually the parasitic moth larva that eats the roots of the agave plant). Mezcal is generally made from the blue agave, but it can also be made from other types of agave. Mezcal may be processed and distilled differently and, unlike tequila, mezcal is not inspected or regulated by the Mexican government. There are some wonderful mezcals, but some can be more like American moonshine, so be careful!

Pulque (pronounced "pool-kae") could very easily be called the grandfather of tequila. It is the awful-tasting, undistilled fermented juice of the agave. Legend has it that centuries before the Spanish came to Mexico, lightning lit a wild agave plant on fire, cooking the piña and leaving its juices to ferment into a strong alcoholic liquid. The ancient Mexican Indians drank this liquid and, as a result, had great hallucinations that they reported to their priests. The priests then tried the vino agave, believed it allowed them to communicate with the gods, and proceeded to use the beverage for medicinal and religious purposes. The Spanish arrived and realized that the bitter juice was stronger than the wine they had brought with them; in an attempt to improve the flavor, they distilled it—not once but twice. Hence, eventually, tequila. To this day, pulque is still sold and imbibed in Mexico, although most of it is not actually made from the highly coveted blue agave plant. There is no government control of pulque—so again, be careful!

As with fine wines, whiskies, or brandies (and a lot else besides), with tequila, you get what you pay for. You pay more for better quality. This means that 100 percent blue agave tequilas are more expensive. But, not to worry. You don't need superpremium tequila to make a great margarita. After all, who can afford to have Chateau Margaux or Opus One with dinner every night? Don't count on using 100 percent agave tequila every time you have a margarita. Close to half of the margaritas in this book, including Maria's Special, our house margarita, use premium tequila. If you follow our recipes, you won't be disappointed.

Whose Tequila Is It Anyway?

The saying goes that tequila was discovered by the people of Mexico hundreds of years ago, but it was only discovered by Americans in the 1990s! Oh, tequila has been trickling into the United States for a long time, ever since José Cuervo delivered the first batch to New Mexico back at the turn of the century. Herradura was the first 100 percent agave super-premium tequila to be imported into the United States, and it still has a well-established base of sales that is hard to discount. But in the late 1980s and early 1990s, there were two Americans who set the ball rolling for the U.S. tequila marketing boom: Bob Denton and Martin Crowley.

Bob Denton perhaps has influenced the superpremium tequila importing industry more than anyone else in the country. Denton, together with his partner Marilyn Smith, had a good deal of success importing and marketing Chinaco tequila back in the 1980s—it achieved cult status and was a favorite of rock stars, among others. Bob was sailing along selling all the Chinaco his Mexican associates could produce when the bottom fell out! The Chinaco plant in Mexico closed down; rumors vary as to the reason, rang-ing from a family fight for control to the more colorful story that Mexican mobsters had shut it down by destroying the distillery and hijacking truckloads of the finished product.

Regardless, there was no more Chinaco coming into the United States; the little that was left was warehoused by Denton or was on dealers' shelves (mostly in California). Why is human nature such that when we *can't* have some-thing, we *must* have it? Such was the case with Chinaco tequila. Everyone wanted Chinaco. The price went through the ceiling. If Chinaco had been a cult thing earlier, it became a legend now.

But there was no more Chinaco. So, being the smart entrepreneur that he is, Bob Denton contracted with long-time tequila maker Don Felipe Camarena to allow him to market his 100 percent agave Tequila Tapatío in the United States under the "El Tesoro de Don Felipe" label. Denton personally took this estate-grown, -distilled, and -bottled superpremium tequila throughout the United States and introduced it to bars, restaurants, and distributors. Perhaps unknowingly, Denton had established the benchmark for superpremium tequila imported into the United States.

While Denton was extolling the virtues of "the treasure" (El Tesoro) of fine estate-grown 100 percent agave tequila, Martin Crowley was making a deal with the makers of

Siete Leguas tequila to produce a 100 percent agave silver and añejo tequila that he could import and market in the United States under the name of "Patrón." Now, once the deal was consummated, Crowley took a giant step forward: he created a never-before-seen package for his tequila. He presented the tequila in a handblown glass decanter bottle with a ball-shaped stopper that by design would catch the eye of consumers in the United States. Not only did his packaging work, but he had (like Denton, perhaps unknowingly) established the benchmark for the new age of packaging tequila—in unusual handblown, interesting-looking glass bottles.

After a brief distribution arrangement with the Seagrams Company, during the late 1990s Crowley went back in-house for his distribution. Crowley died in 2002, leaving the Patrón management and distribution to his longtime partner, Paul Mitchell, the cosmetics guru.

Denton did a similar distribution deal with Jim Beam during the mid-1990s, but ended up selling his El Tesoro import rights to Beam. Denton retired from the tequila importing business, but not before he resurrected Chinaco.

These two pioneers have been instrumental in raising customer awareness of truly exceptional, superpremium (100 percent agave) tequila, and their role in making tequila the fastest-growing liquor is to be applauded.

This progression leads us to reemphasize something you really need to be careful about when buying tequila: if it is expensive, first make sure the tequila is 100 percent agave. Second, make sure you're not paying for the bottle. Some of the great tequilas being sold in America today are packaged in great-looking handblown glass bottles, and just because the bottle may be unusual, don't shy away from it. Refer to the tequila descriptions later in this book or ask your liquor dealer about it—most dealers are becoming more and more familiar with superpremium tequilas and can give intelligent guidance to their customers.

Where Is Tequila Today, and Where's It Going to Be Tomorrow?

This second edition of *The Great Margarita Book* features forty-nine new tequilas and says goodbye to thirty-nine others. That's quite a turnover. Here's what happened.

The success of Denton and Crowley became known in the United States (and Mexico), and one by one, entrepreneurs went to Jalisco seeking out deals with Mexican tequila distillers. They assured producers that they would distribute and market their tequilas in the United States in terrific new bottles that would surpass anything that had gone before. They convinced Mexican producers to let them import the product under a new name or even the same name used in Mexico.

Some worked. Some didn't. Most of those that worked are in this edition of *The Great Margarita Book*. Among those tequilas that are no longer being imported is Porfidio, whose production problems and sales falloff led to its demise. The stars are still El Tesoro, Patrón, and the original superpremium tequila imported into the United States, Herradura. The tequila powerhouses, José Cuervo and Sauza, have fortified their hold on the American market by continuing to produce quality mixtos as well as adding premium 100 percent agaves in all price ranges.

Tequila has gained enough respect since the late 1980s to demand as much as several hundred dollars a bottle. The great crystal wineglass manufacturer, Riedel, has created a crystal tequila tasting glass that is revolutionary. Compare the Riedel tequila tasting glass to a regular shot glass or snifter by pouring an ounce of superpremium tequila in each one. The difference in taste with the Riedel tasting glass is unbelievable.

The latest brouhaha in tequiladom is the Mexican government wanting to require that all tequila be bottled in Mexico. Currently, only 100 percent agave tequilas are required to be bottled in Mexico. A big percentage of mixtos are now shipped to bottling plants in the United States in barrels or even tanker cars. The only certainty in the tequila business is that the Mexican government has realized that tequila is the jewel of Mexican exports and they are committed to maintaining the quality of the product.

CHAPTER TWO

Other Essentials for a Great Margarita

A great margarita—a real margarita—must contain three primary ingredients: real tequila, real orange liqueur, and real freshly squeezed lemon or lime juice. It must also be correctly hand shaken with ice, not put into a blender. Tequila drinks mixed in a blender, using extra sugar, concentrated lime juice, frozen lemonade, limeade, or a commercial margarita mix, are not real margaritas no matter how good the tequila is. Nothing bothers me more than to see a bar serving margaritas (most likely made using a lot of ice, sugar, water, and cheap rotgut tequila) out of a slush-type machine right into the glass. These are not real margaritas!

The variations among the margaritas in this book are created by using different tequilas, different orange liqueurs, and different types of citrus juices to make a real margarita.

The Liqueur

Margaritas are made using one of three different orange liqueurs: triple sec, Cointreau, or Grand Marnier. The combinations of different liqueurs with the many different kinds of tequilas yield a wide variety of subtle variations on the basic margarita.

Triple sec is a clear liqueur made from the skins of Curaçao and other exotic oranges that have been fermented, sun dried, reconstituted in distilled water, and then triple distilled. Each of the distillations condenses the natural sugars and removes some of the bitterness of the orange peel. Most commercial triple sec is artificially flavored; be sure to check the label to find one made with all-natural ingredients. Triple secs are usually available in 60 proof or 42 proof. At Maria's we prefer the lower-alcohol-content version with the delicate flavor of tequila. We use Bols brand 42-proof triple sec for several of our margaritas. Bols is a premium-quality triple sec, as are Marie Brizard and DeKuyper.

Cointreau is a superpremium, 80-proof orange liqueur imported from France. It was created in 1849 by Adolphe Cointreau and his brother Edouard, who were candy makers experimenting with fruit and spirits. (It was probably the orange liqueur used to make the original margarita.) Cointreau is a blend of bitter and sweet oranges, grown and selected for their quality in Haiti, Brazil, and Spain. The only part of the orange that is used is the peel, which is laid out to dry in the sun for several days, then sent back to the distillery in Angers, France. There the oil from the peels is blended with grain neutral spirits and pure cane sugar and distilled three times. Cointreau's distinctive orange flavor is usually the best complement to premium or superpremium tequila. I wouldn't think of using anything other than Cointreau or Grand Marnier with superpremium tequila.

Grand Marnier, another French import, is made by blending superpremium orange liqueur with premium cognac, which is then aged for a minimum of eighteen months. At Maria's, we use Grand Marnier to make our Grand Gold Margarita (see page 38), one of the most popular of all our margaritas. Grand Marnier is 80 proof.

If you want a margarita with a lot of character and a completely different "twist," make it with Grand Marnier. The subtle flavor of oranges blends with the hint of cognac and the flavor of the tequila to make quite a statement! However, because the flavor of the Grand Marnier can easily become the dominant flavor of the drink, margaritas made with Cointreau are probably as authentic as you'll want to get. But you can decide for yourself what you like—there are an awful lot of folks that love margaritas made with Grand Marnier.

The Citrus Juice

Based on research we have done on the origins of the margarita (see chapter 3), I am confident that the original margarita was indeed made with freshly squeezed lime juice. Having said that, I must admit that we use freshly squeezed lemon juice at Maria's.

The reason we use lemon juice is that the quality of fresh limes is just too inconsistent. Depending on the season, we sometimes get limes from Mexico, at other times from California, Florida, or South America, and we are always at the mercy of our suppliers. Sometimes those limes can be so tart you can't stand them, while at other times they'll be as sweet as sugar. By contrast, lemons are considerably more uniform in flavor, regardless of geographical origin or time of year. If you do find a sweet, juicy lime, we'll bet that you can tell little difference in flavor between a margarita made with lemon juice and one made with lime juice. (We do not recommend frozen concentrated lime or lemon juice that has sugar added, but Minute Maid produces a pure, frozen unsweetened lemon juice that may be substituted for fresh.)

We never use commercial margarita mix at Maria's, and we strongly recommend that you avoid it too. We use a commercial sweet-and-sour mix in a margarita only when a customer insists that his or her margarita be frozen and mixed in the blender instead of shaken. The problem with using a blender to make margaritas is that the ice turns to water and overdilutes the cocktail, making it almost flavorless. As convinced as we are at Maria's about what makes a real margarita, we also believe that the customer is always right—even when he or she isn't. So if you want a frozen margarita at Maria's, we will make it for you.

The Salt

Salt is an important element of the margarita. It is never put in the drink itself—it is only used on the rim of the margarita glass. You simply pass a wedge of lemon or lime over the rim of an empty glass, then dip the glass in a saucer of salt.

We use kosher salt because it is additive free and because the coarser texture has the best consistency. Simple table salt is acceptable, although you will need more of it and it will dissolve quickly. (If using table salt, use less lemon or lime juice on the rim of the glass so that less salt will stick to it.) Inexpensive boxes of kosher salt are available at most grocery stores and will last a very long time.

The Ice

One of the most important ingredients in a real margarita is the ice. The shape and size of the ice cubes are important because, as you shake the margarita, the corners of the ice cubes will break off and dilute the other ingredients to just the proper point. "Round ice cubes" are not only an oxymoron, they just don't work in a margarita (they will work, however, if you crack each one). Be careful, since the more you crack and crush your ice, the more you'll dilute your margarita.

You need to use small cubes, ideally about 1 inch (a little smaller will do, but not too much larger than that). If you're using ice out of household refrigerator ice trays, crack it into pieces by tapping the cubes sharply with the back of a tablespoon while cradling them in the palm of your cupped hand. The ideal ice is the commercial type you buy in bags at most grocery, liquor, or convenience stores.

The Equipment

Real margaritas are pretty low-tech, and (you'll be glad to hear) the equipment needed to make them requires little capital. The first things you'll need are a stainless steel cocktail shaker top and a 16-ounce cocktail shaker. Shaking the mixture of tequila, orange liqueur, lemon juice, and ice will break off just the right amount from the corners of the ice for proper dilution of the drink.

Please don't use a blender! All it does is puree everything into a watery slush, diluting the flavor of the tequila and the orange liqueur. The result is a pale version of a margarita that bears little resemblance to the real thing and is a waste of good liquor. The one and only exception to this rule is when making fruit margaritas. Although they're not true margaritas, these are wonderful, refreshing summertime drinks, and sometimes you just can't beat the taste of fresh strawberries, peaches, or apricots. A blender or food processor is a must for making these; just follow the recipes we have provided.

We recommend that margaritas be served on the rocks (over ice). We don't think you'll mind the small amount of dilution that occurs during the time it takes to consume your margarita. The drink stays colder longer, and the water added from the melting ice will not affect the flavor of the margarita.

If you prefer your margaritas "up," or without ice, you'll need some sort of a drink strainer (you've probably seen one of those stainless steel things behind the bar that looks like a miniature Ping-Pong paddle with a spring around it). Some of the bartenders at Maria's prefer to strain margaritas by inserting the bottom of the empty shaker top into the shaker glass with the cocktail mixture and pouring the liquid out into a glass. If you do this, you won't need a strainer (which makes a cheap alternative).

We do not serve pitchers of margaritas at Maria's for several reasons that have to do with the practical concerns of running a restaurant. For one thing, margaritas are quite potent. Each one contains a double shot of 80-proof spirits in a drink so smooth and flavorful that when properly made it just goes down too easily. If we served entire pitchers of margaritas, we would have a bunch of drunk customers, and that is not our goal. Moreover, an entire pitcher of margaritas sitting on a table would become so diluted from the melted ice that the intended flavor of the margaritas would be destroyed. With that in mind, the only feasible way to maintain the integrity of the margarita's flavor in a pitcher would be to serve it with no ice in the pitcher. If you shook eight margaritas individually and strained out the ice, a 64-ounce pitcher (most of our recipes yield about 8 ounces of liquid each) of one of our premium margaritas would cost over $60 (there are not going to be a lot of takers).

We have had success serving numerous margaritas at one time while maintaining the flavor by following a simple procedure using a large punch bowl. (Every year, we serve our La Ultima Margarita to over 1,000 people at the Santa

Fe Buckaroo Ball and receive rave reviews!) To use a punch bowl, simply add a large chunk of ice (not cubes) after all of the ingredients are in the bowl and well mixed. Then stir to create a bit of melting. Using a ladle, pour the margarita mixture into salt-rimmed glasses that have been filled at least three-quarters full with ice cubes. The chunk of ice will add the proper amount of water to the concoction; however, if the flavor is a bit tart, add a cup or two of cold water until you get the taste you desire.

If you are entertaining at home and *do* choose to serve by the pitcher, you can hand shake individual margaritas according to the recipe and strain off the liquid into a chilled pitcher until it's as full as you want it to be. Have an ice bucket handy, along with salt-rimmed glasses. Add the ice to the presalted glasses and pour the margarita from the pitcher. Just remember, half the fun is shaking each cocktail—it's a great way to show off!

We use two different types of glasses for our margaritas. One is the hurricane-style stemmed glass, which is curved like the glass chimney of hurricane lamps; the other is the flat saucer-type stemmed glass often used for champagne. The hurricane glass is used for margaritas on the rocks, and the saucer-type is used for "up" margaritas.

Any variation of these glasses will do, and the Margarita Police will not hunt you down or press charges if you use a stemless glass. The main requirement is that your glass be big enough to hold the margarita. As we like to put it, "It ain't what you drink from, it's what you're drinking" (or words to that effect).

The only other piece of equipment you will need is a jigger or other measuring device. All our recipes list the ingredients as ounces or fractions of an ounce (basic bar jiggers come in $3/4$-ounce, 1-ounce, $1^1/2$-ounce, and 2-ounce sizes). We recommend that you buy a combination stainless steel jigger with one side measuring $3/4$ ounce, the other $1^1/4$ ounces (you can double the $3/4$-ounce side for $1^1/2$ ounces, etc.). These jiggers look like hourglasses and should be available at most gourmet-cooking or bar-supply stores. If all else fails, just remember that $3/4$ ounce equals $1^1/2$ tablespoons, 1 ounce equals 2 tablespoons, and $1^1/4$ ounces equals $2^1/2$ tablespoons.

CHAPTER THREE

The Noble Origins of the Margarita

Who invented the margarita? One might just as easily ask, "Who discovered fire?" The point is, someone, sometime, took the plunge and made a margarita. And, while not as old as fire, its flavor is unique unto itself.

There are several stories (or legends, if you will) as to the origin of the margarita. In order to cover all the bases, we asked a number of food and beverage magazines to print a request for readers' versions of the margarita story. We were surprised both by the number of responses and by the variety of theories out there. Far be it from us to say which story is true; instead, we would like to pass along the most interesting stories so you can come to your own conclusion. The accounts are given in their original versions.

The most commonly related story of the margarita's origin is this one:

Shortly after World War II, corporate America (and Hollywood) discovered Palm Springs, California, as a pleasant and scenic retreat from the hustle and bustle of the big city: play some golf, talk some business, and enjoy some good liquor with the boys. Well, Palm Springs is only a few hours' drive from Mexico and, with this close proximity, a magical "new" liquor, tequila, was discovered by affluent America.

These corporate guys were introduced to tequila the old-fashioned way: a shot of tequila, a lick of salt, and a bit of lime—brings tears to your eyes, doesn't it? The same "good old boys" then started bringing their wives and girlfriends (and no doubt in some cases both) to their little getaway out in the middle of the California desert and, like most men, they wanted to impress the womenfolk with their newly discovered tequila and their macho way of drinking it. Sorry, boys: the shot of tequila, lick of salt, and bite of lime wasn't the ladies' cup of tea.

So along came Jones or Garcia (or whomever—history does not record the creative genius in this version) who concocted a drink that had all of the same elements of the shot of tequila—the liquor, the salt, and the lime—except that Cointreau was added to give the cocktail a little sweetness. This enterprising mixologist created the first margarita by shaking the essential ingredients in a shaker glass over ice, then straining the cocktail into a salt-rimmed glass.

Not only did the women love it, but so did the guys. Although this legend does not name the bartender responsible, it does record that he named his creation after his girlfriend, Margarita. Or, who knows—perhaps the bartender was named Margarita!

Another theory submitted by an advertising agency (published in the fall 1991 edition of the Taylor/Christian Advertising Agency magazine, *!deas*) identifies a specific woman named Margarita. You probably will not be too surprised to learn that Taylor/Christian Advertising was the agency of record for Cointreau when they published this story:

According to legend, it was during a party at [Margarita Sames's] cliff-side hacienda in Acapulco in 1948 when Margarita began experimenting with "the drink." Cointreau was the key ingredient, and today she scoffs at recipes that call for triple sec. At the party was a group of her closest friends, among them Nicky Hilton of the Hilton Hotel legacy. . . . Margarita was looking for something to cut the dust of a hot December afternoon in Mexico when she stumbled upon "something that kept the party going for two weeks." Margarita's original recipe called for three parts tequila to one part Cointreau and one part lime juice, but being cognizant of America's concern with alcohol, the agency asked her for permission to weaken the mixture. "Okay, as long as you don't use triple sec or blend it up like a Tastee Freeze," she replied tersely. To enjoy Margarita's original Margarita, blend one part tequila, one part fresh lime juice, and one part Cointreau in a shaker of ice. Shake vigorously and pour into a lightly salted glass. Anything else is not the Sames. And, according to Margarita, "not worth its salt."

We heard directly from the folks at Cointreau when they learned about our quest for the origin of the margarita, and they sent us the letter on the next page. (Note the date of the letter—clever, huh? Especially since we sent out our call for margarita legends almost fifty years later! Whether the contents of the letter are true or not, you have to admire Cointreau's enterprising publicity department!)

An article from the July 1991 *Texas Monthly* (submitted by Patrick O'Rourke of Rémy Amerique in Sacramento, California—the U.S. distributor of Cointreau) discusses Mrs. Sames's claim. It also mentions that the owner of the Tail o' the Cock, a Los Angeles restaurant and bar, was a houseguest of Mrs. Sames, hence the theory that the margarita originated there. (The Tail o' the Cock has also been mentioned in other margarita-origin stories.)

This Associated Press obituary, submitted by Evelyn Greenwald of the Los Angeles Public Library's State of California Answer Network, appeared in newspapers all over the country in October 1992:

Dateline: San Diego (AP)—Carlos Herrera, known locally as the man who topped a tequila concoction with salt and called it a Margarita, has died. He was 90. Herrera died Monday at Grossmont Hospital. His daughter, Gloria Amezcua, said he died of natural causes. Herrera's relatives say he invented the drink at Rancho La Gloria, a restaurant he

July 13, 1948

Dear Mr. Lucero,

Greetings from Acapulco! Sorry you can't be with us now to enjoy the sunny weather.

Here's a little memento to let you know I'm thinking of you and to tell you about this wonderful new concoction I created. I hope you'll try it yourself. It's delightful! When you taste it, I'll bet you'll feel like you're here.

Last Christmas, I wanted to give my guests something new and very special, so I mixed equal parts of Cointreau (my favorite liqueur), my best tequila and lime juice and served it in champagne glasses with just a dusting of salt on the rims. Everyone raved about "the drink," and how the smooth orange flavor of Cointreau blended with tequila and tart lime juice made a very refreshing cocktail. They all said they'd never tasted anything like it. It just made our holiday celebration!

The best part is that just last week, my husband Bill said we can't call it "the drink" forever, so he presented me with two lovely glasses etched with "Margarita." "Now 'the drink' has a name," he said. Wasn't that sweet?

Try my original, The Original Margarita made with Cointreau. I'm sure you'll find it as special as we all do.

Fondly,
Margarita

P.S. Keep the frame on your desk to remind you of the special times you'll always have with The Original Margarita.

opened in 1935 at his home south of Tijuana. He told friends that it was sometime in 1938 or '39 that he decided to mix a jigger of white tequila with lemon juice, shaved ice, triple sec and—the crowning touch—salt. Local legend has it that one of his customers was a showgirl and some-time actress who called herself Marjorie King. She was allergic to all hard liquor except tequila, and she didn't like to drink that straight. That reputedly sent Herrera to experimenting, and he named the result "Margarita" after the actress, the legend goes.

We thank Thomas Kandziora, the bar manager of the American Legion Post #288 in Cedarburg, Wisconsin, who sent us an abridged version of this article from the *Chicago Tribune*, and Mary Louise Rogers of San Diego, who sent a similar article that ran in the *San Diego Tribune*. Mary Louise adds:

I believe this story must have some merit as I remember after arriving in San Diego late in 1958, friends and I made the trek to Rosarito Beach for lobster. There was a favorite bar we stopped at on the old road on our way down, and that was where I first drank a margarita.

Although Herrera was given local credit for the frosty drink, several others have claimed to have invented the mar-garita, according to *The Dictionary of American Food and Drink* by John F. Mariani, published in 1983. The book doesn't name Herrera, but it says one story traces the birth of the margarita to an unidentified creator near the Caliente Racetrack in the 1930s, the place and time Herrera claimed he first mixed a margarita. (Hmmm . . . we wonder if Mr. Herrera ever worked at a bar at the Caliente Racetrack or in Palm Springs.)

Food writer Colman Andrews sent us this contribution regarding the origin of the margarita:

I think I know what inspired it: the classic '30s cocktail called the Sidecar. The Sidecar was supposedly invented in 1931 at the legendary Harry's New York Bar on the Rue Daunou in Paris. The story is that it was created, and named, for a young American millionaire—there always seems to be a young American millionaire involved in tales of this sort—who liked to tour the drinking places of the French capital in the sidecar of a friend's motorcycle.

As you may well know, the Sidecar is classically made with two ounces of cognac, 1/2 ounce of fresh-squeezed lemon juice, and 1/4 ounce of Cointreau. These ingredients are shaken together with cracked ice and strained into a cocktail glass whose rim has been dipped in sugar. By sim-ply replacing the cognac with tequila and the sugar with salt, you'd have a pretty reasonable Margarita—and I'd bet that some old-school bartender who knew the Sidecar, and who perhaps had traveled to Mexico where tequila might otherwise be consumed with salt and lime on the side, put various elements together and came up with this classic drink.

I have several cocktail manuals from the 1950s, incidentally, in which neither the Margarita nor tequila itself is mentioned, suggesting that, whenever it might have been invented, it certainly hadn't yet become a standard drink at that time in the United States. Though I'm sure it was around before this, the earliest reference I can find to it in my own library is from the Time-Life volume Wines and Spirits, published in 1968. You might be amused to hear that, in the course of describing the drink, author Alec Waugh states, "Tequila is not a drink that is ever very likely to be popular among Northerners, whose palates have not been hardened by the unrestrained use of chili."

Nicholas Colletti of Pittsburgh, a keen collector of food facts, wrote to us with his theory about the origin of the margarita:

The Margarita was invented by Red Hinton, a bartender in an early Virginia City bar. He named the drink after Margarita Mendes, his Mexican girlfriend. One day, she hit a man over the head with a bottle of whiskey, and his friend, Robert Arthur, got excited and shot off his revolver to scare her away. He accidentally hit her in the top of the head and killed her. However, he was freed, as it was decided that if he had wanted to kill her, he would have aimed at the area that was easiest to hit—her widest area—which in her case happened to be her chest.

The recipe for the original Margarita was as follows: Wet the rim of a glass with the juice of a lemon. Place the rim in a bowl containing salt so the salt sticks to the rim. Put 1 ounce of tequila in a shaker or bowl. Add ½ ounce lemon juice and ½ ounce orange juice. Mix well and pour into the glass. There was no triple sec or ice used to make this drink; there wasn't any in Virginia City when this drink was invented.

Margee Drews from Corona del Mar, California, wrote to tell us:

I have heard many times that Larry J. Cane, former owner and president of El Torito restaurants, "invented" the blended Margarita as we know it. I've heard that he and a bartender, Barry, blended up a batch in a "slush" type machine. That was over thirty years ago in Los Angeles. [Sorry, Margee—that's not a real margarita; it's a slushee!]

The following information, submitted by Raymond Ritter of Westlake, Ohio, is from The Tequila Book by Marion Gorman and Felipe P. de Alba (Contemporary Books, 1978). One of the theories given regarding the origin of the margarita claims that Danny Negrete, the manager of the Crespo Hotel in Pueblo, Mexico, created the drink in 1936 for his girlfriend, Margarita:

She habitually took a dab of salt with whatever she had to drink. Danny decided that he would create a drink for her so she could enjoy it without having to reach into the common table salt-bowl; he would put the salt on the rim of her glass. He chose tequila—probably that was Margarita's favorite drink. Then he decided to add Cointreau and lemon juice and shake it up with ice.

Another theory from the same source names Doña Bertha, owner of a bar in Taxco, Mexico, as the creator of the margarita.

Former Santa Fe restaurateur Walt McDowell wrote to us from Fort Myers, Florida, with a colorful and historical theory:

The sixteenth-century explorer Ponce de Leon traveled to the New World in search of the Fountain of Youth, said to be guarded by a race of ageless giants, the Calusa. While the Fountain of Youth was a myth, the Calusa were indeed a tribe that existed in Florida, and who were not only tall (over six feet) but lived to an estimated eighty to ninety years of age. It is documented that the Calusa, who were trading partners with the Mayan civilization of Mexico, were versed in the cultivation of many tropical fruits, including sweet limes.

In 1513, Ponce de Leon made contact with the Calusa but later died in a war he fought against them. Two hundred years later, Ponce de Leon's direct descendant, Margerete, was the wife of a well-known pirate, Don José Gaspar, whose trading booty in the Gulf of Mexico included "cactus whisky," distilled from the agave plant and now known as tequila. Gaspar's favorite drink was sweet lime juice and "cactus whiskey," with a touch of sea salt left on the rim of the mug after it had been washed in sea water. This potion was named by his crew after his wife, Margerete.

Elaine Corn, aptly named food critic, writer, and author, wrote to let us know about Francisco "Pancho" Morales, a bartender from Juarez who claimed to have invented the margarita in 1942:

He [Morales] plied his trade at Tommy's Place, a spot popular with Fort Bliss GIs. This is where the Margarita supposedly first was poured, despite claims to its origin as frequent as Elvis sightings. The first thing to dispel is this: It wasn't named for a woman or child. A 1974 article in Texas Monthly magazine written by El Pasoan Brad Cooper ought to have been the last word on the subject, so thorough is the depiction. Pancho Morales is presented as the clear creator, with paper documentation, convenient timing, and oral testimony. Still, Cooper carefully constructs his article liberally using the term "supposedly" in almost every reference to anything having to do with the Margarita. . . .

"A lady came in and ordered a Magnolia," Morales told Cooper. The only thing Morales knew about a Magnolia—a true drink known in Juarez bars—was that it had Cointreau, a little lime and some kind of liquor. So, he did what any good bartender would do: He winged it. The woman recognized the fake, but said it was good anyway, probably because Morales had loaded it with enough tequila to make anyone smile. Morales' train of thought had gone to flowers, from magnolia to daisy, which translates in Spanish to Margarita.

The following story was submitted by Ronnie Vaughan, a sales executive for the Albuquerque distributor of José Cuervo tequila. It's from the Cuervo "fact book" provided to salespeople for the National Distributing Company:

Margaritas originated "in heaven," say its most devoted admirers. Other versions of the story vary. One of the best claims has been staked by the Tail o' the Cock restaurant on La Cienega in Los Angeles. The year: 1954. The culprit: the head bartender. The result: if this was indeed a first, a place in beverage history.

A similar story was provided by Lee Spencer:

After the war, Young's Market Company owner Vernon Underwood owned a tequila brand called José Cuervo. They were and still are a major liquor distributor in Los Angeles. At that time, vodka was start-ing to move due to a popular drink made famous at the Cock and Bull restaurant on Sunset Boulevard, Los Angeles, called Moscow Mule. Underwood took his tequila to his friend McHenry, who owned the Tail o' the Cock restaurant. They gave it to his bartender, who put together a concoction using lime juice and Curaçao. The results were great, so a name was needed. They asked the bartender, who said: "My wife's name is Margaret. Why not call it a Margarita, Spanish for Margaret?" The rest is history.

An article submitted by Dennis Hamann, printed in a beverage trade magazine in 1969, mentions the same Vernon Underwood, then-president of the Young Market Company. In this version, Underwood was curious to know why the Tail o' the Cock restaurant was suddenly ordering five cases of tequila at a time, during a period when tequila sales were relatively dormant. He found that the bartender had invented the margarita, using Underwood's Cuervo tequila, and that this cocktail was rapidly winning acclaim by word of mouth. As a result, Underwood's company launched the first tequila advertising campaign with the theme "Marga-rita is more than just a girl's name," with emphasis on the fact that the jet set had taken to drinking margaritas in posh surroundings wearing white ties and tails.

Another article submitted by Glen "The Bartender" Steward, from Las Vegas, Nevada, repeats the claim that Carlos Herrera (see page 21) invented the margarita and named it after a showgirl, Marjorie King (although in this version, Herrera's first name is Danny). The article then quotes Herrera as saying, "The Mexican bartender at the Tail o' the Cock in Los Angeles was a friend, and I told him how to make it [the margarita]. . . . One day I walked in there and he said, 'Danny, look around. Everybody's drinking Margaritas.'"

Could this be the missing link between all these stories?

There are probably two or three dozen more stories about how the margarita was invented. You might even know one of them. One problem in pinning down the origins of the margarita is that, whatever you name the drink, tequila mixes so naturally and appealingly with citrus juices that it was bound to happen sooner or later, and perhaps sooner even than we think. The bottom line is, the margarita was invented and, with some variations, it is the same (or we think it is the same) as it has been since the late 1930s (or late '40s, depending on whom you believe). It is significant that one common denominator in all the margarita stories is the fact that no sugars are ever used, only unsweetened citrus juices. Regardless of what type of margarita you are making, the sweetness should consist solely of the natural sweetness of the blue agave nectar that has been fermented and double distilled into tequila and the orange liqueur that is mixed with it.

CHAPTER FOUR

Recipes for Real Margaritas

The great margarita recipes in this chapter are the formulas we use at Maria's New Mexican Kitchen in Santa Fe. Although the mixing procedure is essentially the same for each margarita, the tequila and orange liqueur—or combination of the two—change from recipe to recipe. That's what gives each margarita its own character and identity.

For small batches (two, three, or four margaritas), squeeze your own fresh lemons. For large batches, we suggest purchasing a quality, commercially produced, freshly squeezed lemon juice. Be sure to use only 100 percent lemon juice with no sugar or preservatives added. If the juice is too tart, dilute it with a bit of cold water.

We suggest that you avoid commercial margarita mixes with all of our recipes. The fresh citrus juice is what makes our Maria's margaritas distinctive (and it will be your claim to fame as well). Don't hesitate, however, to also try freshly squeezed lime juice. As a matter of fact, one fun way to entertain with margaritas is to have a blind taste test between margaritas made with freshly squeezed lemon juice and those made with freshly squeezed lime juice. It's amazing how close the final results really are.

As with any recipe, first follow our original recipe, sticking to the measurements suggested. Once you've mastered the original, feel free to tweak the ingredients to your liking. Don't hesitate to increase or decrease the amounts of tequila, liqueur, or citrus juice. Experiment! Make it your own margarita. But remember, never add sugar and never blend it (unless it's a fruit concoction). Blending the ingredients with ice will dilute the margarita so much that it's virtually flavorless and you end up cheating yourself out of the grand new tequila flavors coming from Mexico.

Warning: each margarita calls for the equivalent of a double shot of alcohol. They are smooth and tasty, so you might want to serve food alongside your margaritas like we do. We've included our favorite food and recipe suggestions at the end of the book. Enjoy!

Cuervo

The name José Cuervo is virtually synonymous with tequila. Truly, Cuervo is the world's premier tequila distiller. They produce a wide array of premium and superpremium tequilas and export more than one million cases of tequilas to the United States annually.

During the late 1990s, Cuervo went through a good deal of change. For starters, they changed importers, from Heublein to Diageo. At the same time, Cuervo became very aggressive in terms of competing with the superpremium boutique brands that had been flooding the market. (As a matter of fact, one of the most expensive margaritas on Maria's list, which sells for $32.00, is made with Cuervo Reserva de la Familia.) To everyone's surprise, they went as far as halting production of their Cuervo Silver, one of the best-selling tequilas in the United States.

Cuervo has introduced Cuervo Clásico, a young mixto tequila in the silver style, which has replaced their Silver (or Blanco) tequila. Its price point is close to that of Cuervo Especial. (We still use Cuervo Especial, a mixto, to make our house margarita, called Maria's Special Margarita.) They also took the Cuervo name off their 1800 brand and made the 1800 Añejo 100 percent agave (although the 1800 Reposado is still a mixto). The only trace of Cuervo left on the 1800 bottles is their familiar NOM number. Great tequilas, popularly priced (Cuervo's Tradicional 100 percent agave reposado is one of the best buys on 100 percent agave tequila), and available almost anywhere in the world—that's José Cuervo.

MARIA'S SPECIAL MARGARITA
Makes 1 margarita

Maria's Special Margarita is made with José Cuervo Especial and is the number one best-selling hand-shaken margarita in Santa Fe. José Cuervo Especial, commonly called Cuervo gold, is perhaps the best known of all tequilas sold in the United States—it's the one that Jimmy Buffett refers to in his classic "Margaritaville" recording.

1 lemon or lime wedge
Saucer of kosher salt (about ¼ inch deep)
1¼ ounces José Cuervo Especial tequila
1 ounce Bols triple sec
1½ ounces freshly squeezed lemon or lime juice
Ice

Run the lemon or lime wedge around the rim of a hurricane-style margarita glass. Dip the rim of the glass into the saucer of salt, rotating the rim in the salt until the desired amount has collected on the glass.

Measure the tequila, triple sec, and lemon or lime juice into a 16-ounce cocktail shaker glass full of ice. Place a stainless steel cocktail shaker over the glass, tapping the top to create a seal. Shake vigorously for about 5 seconds and pour into the salt-rimmed glass.

Margarita Tip Anytime you make a margarita, consider the ice very carefully! Ice should be no larger than 1-inch cubes with corners. The corners will break off during the shaking and add the perfect amount of dilution for the drink. Round ice cubes are not the best. Most commercially sold ice cubes are your best bet when entertaining with margaritas.

Tequila Tidbit The United States is the biggest consumer of tequila (even outselling Mexico!), with imports more than double the consumption in Mexico itself. The third-largest consumer of tequila is Greece.

MARIA'S 100 PERCENT AGAVE HOUSE MARGARITA
Makes 1 margarita

We wanted our customers to be able to experience the magic of a margarita using 100 percent agave tequila without it costing an arm and a leg. We first introduced this margarita using Cabrito Blanco, a 100 percent agave tequila, because we were able to buy it at a reasonable cost. Cabrito has since gone away, but by the time it stopped being shipped into the state of New Mexico our 100 percent agave house margarita had become one of our best sellers. We had no choice but to substitute another 100 percent agave tequila. Our final decision was between José Cuervo Tradicional and Sauza Hornitos—both comparably priced and equally outstanding in quality. Because of our longtime relationship with the Cuervo folks, we decided to use Tradicional. Try the recipe, you'll love it. And the cost is really quite good for such a quality margarita.

    1 lemon or lime wedge
    Saucer of kosher salt (about 1/4 inch deep)
    1¼ ounces José Cuervo Tradicional tequila
    1 ounce Bols triple sec
    1½ ounces freshly squeezed lemon or lime juice
    Ice

Run the lemon or lime wedge around the rim of a hurricane-style margarita glass. Dip the rim of the glass into the saucer of salt, rotating the rim in the salt until the desired amount has collected on the glass.

Measure the tequila, triple sec, and lemon or lime juice into a 16-ounce cocktail shaker glass full of ice. Place a stainless steel cocktail shaker over the glass, tapping the top to create a seal. Shake vigorously for about 5 seconds and pour into the salt-rimmed glass.

Margarita Tip You can, if you want, garnish your margarita with a lemon or lime slice, but you really don't need to. In any case, don't use any other garnish as it will impart its taste to the masterpiece you have just created.

Tequila Tidbit Try this tequila. It's not only affordable, but when it's used to make this margarita, you'll love the way the nose of the agave wafts through the ice, and the way the taste of the natural sugars of agave, orange, and lemon hit the palate.

THE CUERVO CLÁSICO MARGARITA
Makes 1 margarita

After about a year's hiatus, José Cuervo came back with a premium mixto in the silver style that they call Cuervo Clásico. It's basically the same flavor as the Cuervo Especial gold mixto, but without the color. It's a great tequila and a good value. We were happy to add it back to our margarita list when it again became available.

> 1 lemon or lime wedge
> Saucer of kosher salt (about ¼ inch deep)
> 1¼ ounces José Cuervo Clásico tequila
> 1 ounce Bols triple sec
> 1½ ounces freshly squeezed lemon or lime juice
> Ice

Run the lemon or lime wedge around the rim of a hurricane-style margarita glass. Dip the rim of the glass into the saucer of salt, rotating the rim in the salt until the desired amount has collected on the glass.

Measure the tequila, triple sec, and lemon or lime juice into a 16-ounce cocktail shaker glass full of ice. Place a stainless steel cocktail shaker over the glass, tapping the top to create a seal. Shake vigorously for about 5 seconds and pour into the salt-rimmed glass.

Tequila Tidbit The Cuervo family produced mezcal before they distilled tequila. Their mezcal business dates from the late 1700s; tequila was introduced in the last half of the 19th century.

THE TURQUOISE TRAIL MARGARITA
Makes 1 margarita

This is the blue one! You've always seen someone else order this when you were out and about in bars and restaurants and wondered what was in it and how it was made. Well, now you'll know. We use our 100 percent agave house tequila, Cuervo Tradicional, and the key ingredient for a blue margarita, Bols Blue Curaçao. Blue Curaçao is merely triple sec that has been dyed blue with food coloring. It's used a lot in exotic Polynesian drinks. The blue does not alter the flavor, so it's just a regular margarita with blue food coloring. But it's fun. Pick up a bottle of Blue Curaçao and experiment with this and other cocktails.

    1 lemon or lime wedge
    Saucer of kosher salt (about ¼ inch deep)
    1¼ ounces José Cuervo Tradicional tequila
    1 ounce Bols Blue Curaçao
    1½ ounces freshly squeezed lemon or lime juice
    Ice

Run the lemon or lime wedge around the rim of a hurricane-style margarita glass. Dip the rim of the glass into the saucer of salt, rotating the rim in the salt until the desired amount has collected on the glass.

Measure the tequila, Blue Curaçao, and lemon or lime juice into a 16-ounce cocktail shaker glass full of ice. Place a stainless steel cocktail shaker over the glass, tapping the top to create a seal. Shake vigorously for about 5 seconds and pour into the salt-rimmed glass.

Tequila Tidbit Most distillers favor used oak barrels for aging tequila because they tend to impact the liquor less. Previous use (often for aging bourbon) has already extracted some of the wood color and flavor, leaving the tequila purer. Cuervo, however, uses only new American and French oak for aging and only uses each barrel 4 times before discarding.

THE RAFAEL MARGARITA
Makes 1 margarita

The Rafael, or "Ralph," is a longtime favorite of Maria's old-timers and was in fact named after a patron named Ralph, who asked our bartender to make a margarita according to this recipe. This margarita differs from the earlier recipes by combining an inexpensive premium gold tequila (José Cuervo Especial) with Cointreau, an expensive super-premium orange liqueur.

    1 lemon or lime wedge
    Saucer of kosher salt (about ¼ inch deep)
    1¼ ounces José Cuervo Especial tequila
    1 ounce Cointreau
    1½ ounces freshly squeezed lemon or lime juice
    Ice

Run the lemon or lime wedge around the rim of a hurricane-style margarita glass. Dip the rim of the glass into the saucer of salt, rotating the rim in the salt until the desired amount has collected on the glass.

Measure the tequila, Cointreau, and lemon or lime juice into a 16-ounce cocktail shaker glass full of ice. Place a stainless steel cocktail shaker over the glass, tapping the top to create a seal. Shake vigorously for about 5 seconds and pour into the salt-rimmed glass.

Margarita Tip As we progress with the margarita recipes in this book, you will notice that while the ingredients remain proportionately consistent, the combinations of ingredients change subtly. For example, we use not only different tequilas, but different combinations with triple sec, Cointreau, or Grand Marnier.

Tequila Tidbit There are many popular songs that extol the virtues of tequila. In the 1950s, the Champs recorded "Tequila." The Eagles are famous for their "Tequila Sunrise," and we've already mentioned Jimmy Buffett's "Margaritaville." There's also Bobby Bare's "Pour Me Another Tequila, Sheila," but perhaps while you sip this particular cocktail, you'd like to hum along with Shelley West's classic, "José Cuervo, You Are a Friend of Mine."

THE 1812 OVERTURE MARGARITA
Makes 1 margarita

The 1812 Overture is made with 1800 Reposado. This mixto is made by José Cuervo, but is currently being marketed without the Cuervo name. It still comes in the familiar decanter bottle that Cuervo has used for years. This tequila mixed with Cointreau is indeed a symphony of flavor.

> 1 lemon or lime wedge
> Saucer of kosher salt (about ¼ inch deep)
> 1¼ ounces 1800 Reposado
> 1 ounce Cointreau
> 1½ ounces freshly squeezed lemon or lime juice
> Ice

Run the lemon or lime wedge around the rim of a hurricane-style margarita glass. Dip the rim of the glass into the saucer of salt, rotating the rim in the salt until the desired amount has collected on the glass.

Measure the tequila, Cointreau, and lemon or lime juice into a 16-ounce cocktail shaker glass full of ice. Place a stainless steel cocktail shaker over the glass, tapping the top to create a seal. Shake vigorously for about 5 seconds and pour into the salt-rimmed glass.

Tequila Tidbit The town of Tequila is located 40 miles northwest of Guadalajara and has a population of 55,000. The name means "lava hill" in the Nahuatl Indian (Aztec) language, but these native people had vanished by 1656, when a Spanish settlement was permanently established. "Lava hill" refers to the fact that the town sits on the lower slopes of an extinct volcano.

THE GRAND GOLD MARGARITA
Makes 1 margarita

We use the same Cuervo Especial gold tequila for this recipe as for the Maria's Special Margarita, but Grand Marnier rather than triple sec. This gives the cocktail a sweeter, more intense flavor.

1 lemon or lime wedge
Saucer of kosher salt (about ¼ inch deep)
1¼ ounces José Cuervo Especial tequila
1 ounce Grand Marnier
1½ ounces freshly squeezed lemon or lime juice
Ice

Run the lemon or lime wedge around the rim of a hurricane-style margarita glass. Dip the rim of the glass into the saucer of salt, rotating the rim in the salt until the desired amount has collected on the glass.

Measure the tequila, Grand Marnier, and lemon or lime juice into a 16-ounce cocktail shaker glass full of ice. Place a stainless steel cocktail shaker over the glass, tapping the top to create a seal. Shake vigorously for about 5 seconds and pour into the salt-rimmed glass.

Tequila Tidbit To understand the scale of the largest producers in the tequila market, it may come as no surprise to learn that over a third of all tequila is produced by the Cuervo distillery. This is twice as much as Sauza, the next-largest producer. In turn, Sauza is twice as large as the third-biggest producer. Cuervo enjoys a 50 percent market share in the United States.

THE JOSÉ CUERVO TRADICIONAL MARGARITA

Makes 1 margarita

Cuervo, the leading tequila producer in the world, has now brought out a limited production of Tequila José Cuervo Tradicional, a superpremium 100 percent agave reposado tequila (aged in oak barrels for at least 60 days). It is wonderfully smooth, with a delightful nose and flavor.

    1 lemon or lime wedge
    Saucer of kosher salt (about ¼ inch deep)
    1¼ ounces José Cuervo Tradicional tequila
    1 ounce Cointreau
    1½ ounces freshly squeezed lemon or lime juice
    Ice

Run the lemon or lime wedge around the rim of a hurricane-style margarita glass. Dip the rim of the glass into the saucer of salt, rotating the rim in the salt until the desired amount has collected on the glass.

Measure the tequila, Cointreau, and lemon or lime juice into a 16-ounce cocktail shaker glass full of ice. Place a stainless steel cocktail shaker over the glass, tapping the top to create a seal. Shake vigorously for about 5 seconds and pour into the salt-rimmed glass.

Margarita Tip At Maria's, we have strong feelings about commercial margarita mixes. Don't waste good money on them when the best ingredients you can use—fresh lemons and limes—cost only pennies per drink.

Tequila Tidbit Each bottle of Cuervo Tradicional is individually numbered. For some time, Cuervo bottled this fine tequila only in 375 ml bottles, but now they are also bottling this tequila in 750 ml and liter bottles.

THE 1800 MASTERPIECE MARGARITA

Makes 1 margarita

Introduced in 1998 as 1800 Añejo, this 100 percent agave tequila is made by José Cuervo but is being marketed under the brand name "1800," with no reference to Cuervo other than the required NOM number. This is indeed one of Cuervo's best efforts. Mix this añejo with Cointreau for a true masterpiece.

1 lemon or lime wedge
Saucer of kosher salt (about ¼ inch deep)
1¼ ounces 1800 Añejo tequila
1 ounce Cointreau
1½ ounces freshly squeezed lemon or lime juice
Ice

Run the lemon or lime wedge around the rim of a hurricane-style margarita glass. Dip the rim of the glass into the saucer of salt, rotating the rim in the salt until the desired amount has collected on the glass.

Measure the tequila, Cointreau, and lemon or lime juice into a 16-ounce cocktail shaker glass full of ice. Place a stainless steel cocktail shaker over the glass, tapping the top to create a seal. Shake vigorously for about 5 seconds and pour into the salt-rimmed glass.

Tequila Tidbit Don't confuse regular 1800 Reposado tequila with the 1800 Añejo. Remember, if a tequila is 100 percent agave, then it has to say so somewhere on the bottle. The 1800 Añejo says it . . . the 1800 Reposado does not.

THE 24-KARAT GOLD RESERVA MARGARITA
Makes 1 margarita

Three hundred and fifty years in the making! We combine 200th-anniversary hand-crafted José Cuervo Reserva de la Familia 100 percent añejo barrel-select tequila with 150th-anniversary Cuvée Speciale Cent Cinquantenaire Grand Marnier (plus freshly squeezed lemon juice) to make this solid-gold concoction. This tequila comes in a handblown bottle inside a colorful wooden box and will rival any cognac for sipping from a brandy snifter.

1 lemon or lime wedge
Saucer of kosher salt (about ¼ inch deep)
1¼ ounces José Cuervo Reserva de la Familia tequila
1 ounce Cuvée Speciale Cent Cinquantenaire
  Grand Marnier
1½ ounces freshly squeezed lemon or lime juice
Ice

Run the lemon or lime wedge around the rim of a hurricane-style margarita glass. Dip the rim of the glass into the saucer of salt, rotating the rim in the salt until the desired amount has collected on the glass.

Measure the tequila, Grand Marnier, and lemon or lime juice into a 16-ounce cocktail shaker glass full of ice. Place a stainless steel cocktail shaker over the glass, tapping the top to create a seal. Shake vigorously for about 5 seconds and pour into the salt-rimmed glass.

Tequila Tidbit The blue agave plant is a succulent and belongs to the lily family. Its full botanical name is **Agave azul Tequilana Weber**, after the botanist (Weber) who classified the plant.

Margarita Tip The ingredients in this margarita are expensive (we sell this margarita for $32 at Maria's), but for that special occasion, it is worth every penny. With a tequila this good on its own, imagine how good the margarita will be . . . and when you add the 150th-anniversary Grand Marnier (also super sippin' stuff), voilà!

Sauza

The Sauza distillery, located in the town of Tequila, Jalisco, is one of the most modern of tequila plants, using cutting-edge cooking and recovery techniques they've developed over the years. Sauza claims that Sauza Blanco tequila is the traditional favorite and largest-selling tequila in Mexico. (Cuervo claims the same about their tequila for the United States.)

In the early 2000s, Sauza changed its entire packaging program and introduced new labels for all the various tequilas they offer. To the best of our knowledge, Sauza has not changed its distilling method, so you'll get the same tequila inside the new bottle.

THE SAUZA SILVER MARGARITA
Makes 1 margarita

Here is one of the best buys in a quality premium mixto tequila. Sauza Blanco has been around "forever"—you can't go wrong with this popularly priced tequila.

> 1 lemon or lime wedge
> Saucer of kosher salt (about ¼ inch deep)
> 1¼ ounces Sauza Blanco tequila
> 1 ounce Bols triple sec
> 1½ ounces freshly squeezed lemon or lime juice
> Ice

Run the lemon or lime wedge around the rim of a hurricane-style margarita glass. Dip the rim of the glass into the saucer of salt, rotating the rim in the salt until the desired amount has collected on the glass.

Measure the tequila, triple sec, and lemon or lime juice into a 16-ounce cocktail shaker glass full of ice. Place a stainless steel cocktail shaker over the glass, tapping the top to create a seal. Shake vigorously for about 5 seconds and pour into the salt-rimmed glass.

Margarita Tip Attention all readers with a sweet tooth! The natural sugars in the ingredients listed in these recipes should be more than enough to satisfy even those with the sweetest of sweet tooths. If you're used to drinking extremely sweet margaritas, however, ours may seem a bit dry to you. But hey, these are real margaritas, so we urge you to try a few of our recipes. We are sure that you'll never stray back to icky-sweet fake margaritas again!

Tequila Tidbit The blue agave plant grows best in the elevated altitude and dry volcanic soil of west-central Mexico. Another major crop in the region is sugarcane, which is also used by some brands in the tequila-making process.

THE SAUZA GOLD MARGARITA
Makes 1 margarita

This margarita is made with one of the most popular tequilas used in Mexico: Sauza Extra Gold. You'll notice that the most reputable distillers, like Sauza, will not try to mislead the public by calling a fresh tequila with caramel coloring "añejo," which derives its golden color from aging in oak barrels.

    1 lemon or lime wedge
    Saucer of kosher salt (about ¼ inch deep)
    1¼ ounces Sauza Extra Gold tequila
    1 ounce Bols triple sec
    1½ ounces freshly squeezed lemon or lime juice
    Ice

Run the lemon or lime wedge around the rim of a hurricane-style margarita glass. Dip the rim of the glass into the saucer of salt, rotating the rim in the salt until the desired amount has collected on the glass.

Measure the tequila, triple sec, and lemon or lime juice into a 16-ounce cocktail shaker glass full of ice. Place a stainless steel cocktail shaker over the glass, tapping the top to create a seal. Shake vigorously for about 5 seconds and pour into the salt-rimmed glass.

Tequila Tidbit Tequila can only be produced in very defined regions of 5 states in Mexico. Only in the state of Jalisco is tequila production allowed throughout the entire state. All 100 percent agave tequila must be produced and bottled in the region of the origin.

THE THREE Gs MARGARITA
Makes 1 margarita

The "Three Gs" in the title refers to Sauza's Tres Generaciones (Three Generations) Añejo tequila, an aged, 100 percent agave tequila produced to honor the successive tequila makers of the Sauza family since 1873: Don Cenobio, Don Eladio, and Don Javier Sauza. This tequila, like all añejos, must be aged in inspector-sealed oak barrels for more than 1 year. Because of this, the tequila is a pale golden color that is acquired naturally from the barrels during the aging process.

    1 lemon or lime wedge
    Saucer of kosher salt (about ¼ inch deep)
    1¼ ounces Sauza Tres Generaciones Añejo tequila
    1 ounce Cointreau
    1½ ounces freshly squeezed lemon or lime juice
    Ice

Run the lemon or lime wedge around the rim of a hurricane-style margarita glass. Dip the rim of the glass into the saucer of salt, rotating the rim in the salt until the desired amount has collected on the glass.

Measure the tequila, Cointreau, and lemon or lime juice into a 16-ounce cocktail shaker glass full of ice. Place a stainless steel cocktail shaker over the glass, tapping the top to create a seal. Shake vigorously for about 5 seconds and pour into the salt-rimmed glass.

Margarita Tip Some bars serve margaritas with a straw. Heck, we do this at Maria's. The straw should be used to stir rather than for sipping the cocktail. Margaritas should be sipped from the rim of the glass, through the salt.

Tequila Tidbit Most aged tequilas are placed in oak barrels (most often old, used Kentucky whiskey barrels) for the aging process. Mexican government inspectors seal these barrels when the tequila is put down and must be present when the seal is broken by the producer to bottle the product.

THE HORNY TOAD MARGARITA
Makes 1 margarita

*Horny toad is slang for "horned toad," a creature found in abundance
in the high desert terrain around Santa Fe. Maria's sells a lot of these
margaritas just because of the name (usually, the wife or girlfriend
orders it while smiling at the husband or boyfriend and saying something
like, "BOY, was this one named after you!"). It also happens to be one
of the best margaritas at Maria's. In Spanish* hornitos *means "little
ovens" and refers to the ovens in which the agave piñas are cooked.*

    1 lemon or lime wedge
    Saucer of kosher salt (about ¼ inch deep)
    1¼ ounces Sauza Hornitos tequila
    1 ounce Cointreau
    1½ ounces freshly squeezed lemon or lime juice
    Ice

Run the lemon or lime wedge around the rim of a hurricane-
style margarita glass. Dip the rim of the glass into the saucer
of salt, rotating the rim in the salt until the desired amount
has collected on the glass.

Measure the tequila, Cointreau, and lemon or lime juice
into a 16-ounce cocktail shaker glass full of ice. Place a stainless steel cocktail shaker over the glass, tapping the top to
create a seal. Shake vigorously for about 5 seconds and pour
into the salt-rimmed glass.

Tequila Tidbit Hornitos is one of Sauza's
oldest and most venerable tequilas. It is a
100 percent blue agave reposado tequila
(aged no less than 3 months and up to 1 year
in oak barrels). Because of the slight aging,
Hornitos reposado is slightly darker in color
than the silver tequila, and as with most
100 percent agave tequila that has been
aged, no artificial coloring has been added. One
of the best buys in a quality 100 percent
agave tequila.

46

THE SAUZA CONMEMORATIVO MARGARITA

Makes 1 margarita

Sauza tequila is the major rival to Cuervo, in terms of volume and market share, and the Conmemorativo was introduced in an attempt to compete with the premium tequilas that Cuervo has been placing in the American market. It is a delightfully smooth añejo tequila, making it difficult to tell that this tequila is not 100 percent blue agave.

> 1 lemon or lime wedge
> Saucer of kosher salt (about ¼ inch deep)
> 1¼ ounces Sauza Conmemorativo tequila
> 1 ounce Cointreau
> 1½ ounces freshly squeezed lemon or lime juice
> Ice

Run the lemon or lime wedge around the rim of a hurricane-style margarita glass. Dip the rim of the glass into the saucer of salt, rotating the rim in the salt until the desired amount has collected on the glass.

Measure the tequila, Cointreau, and lemon or lime juice into a 16-ounce cocktail shaker glass full of ice. Place a stainless steel cocktail shaker over the glass, tapping the top to create a seal. Shake vigorously for about 5 seconds and pour into the salt-rimmed glass.

Margarita Tip Most tequilas are 80 proof (the "proof" is double the percentage of the alcohol in the liquor, so 80 proof means that 40 percent of the volume is alcohol). Triple sec is usually 60 proof, but it can be 42 proof. Cointreau and Grand Marnier are 80 proof. All this means that when you combine tequila with one of these liqueurs, you are serving a double—the same thing as serving a double shot of 80-proof whiskey, for example. So consume margaritas (like all other alcohol) responsibly and in moderation.

Tequila Tidbit Ninety percent of all tequila exported to the United States from Mexico is transported not in the bottle, but by bulk tanker. Most of this tequila is distilled by Cuervo and Sauza.

LO MEJOR DE SAUZA
Makes 1 margarita

Sauza is not to be outdone by the small boutique distillers. Even though they have been exporting their popularly priced 100 percent agave reposado, Hornitos, for some time, they are entering the super-premium market with a big hit, Galardon. Galardon is a quality 100 percent agave reposado tequila that is being marketed in an attractive tin-wrapped bottle boasting that it is "limited production." The other interesting thing about the label is that Sauza is calling Galardon "gran reposado." There is no official designation for "gran reposado." In my opinion, this is the best of all the Sauza line.

    1 lemon or lime wedge
    Saucer of kosher salt (about ¼ inch deep)
    1¼ ounces Sauza Galardon tequila
    1 ounce Cointreau
    1½ ounces freshly squeezed lemon or lime juice
    Ice

Run the lemon or lime wedge around the rim of a hurricane-style margarita glass. Dip the rim of the glass into the saucer of salt, rotating the rim in the salt until the desired amount has collected on the glass.

Measure the tequila, Cointreau, and lemon or lime juice into a 16-ounce cocktail shaker glass full of ice. Place a stainless steel cocktail shaker over the glass, tapping the top to create a seal. Shake vigorously for about 5 seconds and pour into the salt-rimmed glass.

Tequila Tidbit Ancient murals dating back to approximately 200 A.D. can be found at the site of the Great Pyramid of Cholula near Mexico City. These murals depict the Aztec Indians celebrating by drinking what is commonly believed to be the ancestor of modern tequila. It was probably what is now called **pulque**, which is undistilled fermented agave juice.

Margarita Tip When ordering a margarita at a bar or a restaurant, make sure they are using quality ingredients. You may want to specify 100 percent agave tequila (ask the waiter or bartender to show you the bottle) and Cointreau. Most importantly, if they are using a sweet-and-sour or sweetened mix, ask them to instead squeeze lemons or limes for you and shake the drink and serve it on the rocks.

Chinaco

When Chinaco 100 percent agave tequila first arrived in the United States in 1983, it created a new category within the tequila industry. Immediately Chinaco built a reputation for itself among the true connoisseurs of tequila. After the distillery was closed in the late 1980s and the tequila went out of production, Chinaco became the most sought-after tequila ever produced. Then, in the mid-1990s, after super effort, its original importer, Bob Denton, convinced the four sons of the founder, Guillermo Gonzalez, to rekindle La Gonzaleña distillery to once again produce this legendary tequila in very limited quantities. Now in full production, Chinaco is readily available, and because it's distributed by Jim Beam, it should be available most anywhere. The new handblown glass teardrop bottles are very attractive. Chinaco produces only 100 percent agave tequilas and offers a blanco, a reposado, and a well-aged añejo. Chinaco Añejo was first reintroduced to the United States at the 1996 Santa Fe Restaurant Association's Culinary Arts Ball in Santa Fe.

EL CHINACO CLÁSICO MARGARITA

Makes 1 margarita

Maria's Real Margarita List (our menu of margaritas) calls this one "a true delight!" How could it be anything else, given the ingredients? Here we use Chinaco Añejo tequila, which has been carefully aged for up to four years in government-sealed and -certified oak barrels, enriching the tequila with the characteristics and elegance of a fine cognac. Then, we compliment the Chinaco Añejo with not just any Grand Marnier, but the 100th-anniversary Cuvée du Centenaire Grand Marnier. This margarita will cost you nearly $20 at Maria's—try it and see if you think it's worth it.

> 1 lemon or lime wedge
> Saucer of kosher salt (about ¼ inch deep)
> 1¼ ounces Chinaco Añejo tequila
> 1 ounce Cuvée du Centenaire Grand Marnier
> 1½ ounces freshly squeezed lemon or lime juice
> Ice

Run the lemon or lime wedge around the rim of a hurricane-style margarita glass. Dip the rim of the glass into the saucer of salt, rotating the rim in the salt until the desired amount has collected on the glass.

Measure the tequila, Grand Marnier, and lemon or lime juice into a 16-ounce cocktail shaker glass full of ice. Place a stainless steel cocktail shaker over the glass, tapping the top to create a seal. Shake vigorously for about 5 seconds and pour into the salt-rimmed glass.

Tequila Tidbit Only 100 percent agave tequila is required to state the agave percentage on the label. Any other tequila that is at least 51 percent agave does not have to. Some tequilas are obviously more than 51 percent agave, but you'll never know just by reading the label.

EL CHINACO AÑEJO MARGARITA
Makes 1 margarita

The fabled Chinaco tequila first came to the United States in 1983 and was heralded as the most wonderful tequila ever to be imported. Supply couldn't keep up with the demand because, back then, production of superpremium tequila was not a priority. Chinaco quickly became a cult tequila. But then, in the late 1980s, the Chinaco plant closed, making the tequila the most sought-after ever produced. Now, under the guidance of founder Guillermo Gonzalez's four sons, La Gonzaleña distillery in Tamaulipas is once again producing this legendary tequila in very limited quantities. The Chinaco Añejo is the crowning achievement of La Gonzaleña. It is carefully aged for up to four years on oak. Most tequila aficionados will drink this wonderful nectar like a fine cognac, but if you really want a great margarita, just follow this recipe. It's superb!

    1 lemon or lime wedge
    Saucer of kosher salt (about ¼ inch deep)
    1¼ ounces Chinaco Añejo tequila
    1 ounce Cointreau
    1½ ounces freshly squeezed lemon or lime juice
    Ice

Run the lemon or lime wedge around the rim of a hurricane-style margarita glass. Dip the rim of the glass into the saucer of salt, rotating the rim in the salt until the desired amount has collected on the glass.

Measure the tequila, Cointreau, and lemon or lime juice into a 16-ounce cocktail shaker glass full of ice. Place a stainless steel cocktail shaker over the glass, tapping the top to create a seal. Shake vigorously for about 5 seconds and pour into the salt-rimmed glass.

Tequila Tidbit If you hold a tequila-tasting party, code the glasses for a blind tasting and keep score—it's always a good idea to keep notes for future reference. Most importantly, appoint designated drivers in advance if necessary.

EL GRAN CHINACO MARGARITA
Makes 1 margarita

*Mix 100 percent agave Chinaco Reposado tequila and Grand Marnier
with freshly squeezed lemon or lime juice, stick to our recipe, and you'll
come up with one of the most elegant margaritas you've ever tasted. This
one is not for wimps. The cognaclike nature of Chinaco Reposado, which
has been aged for up to one year, combined with the touch of premium
cognac used to fortify the orange liqueur in the Grand Marnier, gives this
margarita a stronger flavor than most of the other recipes in this book.
It may not be as smooth and fruity-sweet as others, but it sure is a
Grand margarita!*

> 1 lemon or lime wedge
> Saucer of kosher salt (about 1/4 inch deep)
> 1 1/4 ounces of Chinaco Reposado tequila
> 1 ounce Grand Marnier
> 1 1/2 ounces freshly squeezed lemon or lime juice
> Ice

Run the lemon or lime wedge around the rim of a hurricane-
style margarita glass. Dip the rim of the glass into the saucer
of salt, rotating the rim in the salt until the desired amount
has collected on the glass.

Measure the tequila, Grand Marnier, and lemon or lime
juice into a 16-ounce cocktail shaker glass full of ice. Place a
stainless steel cocktail shaker over the glass, tapping the top
to create a seal. Shake vigorously for about 5 seconds and
pour into the salt-rimmed glass.

Margarita Tip If you are having a party or plan on serving
margaritas to a large group of people, you may want to presalt
a number of glasses. The way we do it at Maria's (where we
serve as many as 3,000 margaritas in a week) is to place
a clean, thin sponge on a saucer and moisten it with
fresh lemon or lime juice. Turn a glass upside down
and press the rim down on the sponge to moisten it.
Then dip the rim into a saucer of kosher salt and
rotate the rim until the desired amount of salt has
collected on the glass.

Tequila Tidbit Tequila aficionados will tell
you that the superpremium 100 percent
agave tequilas will not give you a hangover.
This is not true for the premium tequilas that
also contain cane sugar.

Herradura

Herradura is estate-bottled by the Romo family in the foothills of the Sierra Madre mountains of Jalisco. The estate dates back to 1870, and Herradura tequila has been produced by five successive generations. Besides being the first superpremium tequila imported into the United States, Herradura Reposado has long served as a quality standard for the Mexican tequila industry.

THE SILVER HERRADURA MARGARITA
Makes 1 margarita

Herradura was one of the first 100 percent agave tequilas imported into the United States and is still the number one–selling superpremium brand in the country.

> 1 lemon or lime wedge
> Saucer of kosher salt (about ¼ inch deep)
> 1¼ ounces Herradura Silver tequila
> 1 ounce Bols triple sec
> 1½ ounces freshly squeezed lemon or lime juice
> Ice

Run the lemon or lime wedge around the rim of a hurricane-style margarita glass. Dip the rim of the glass into the saucer of salt, rotating the rim in the salt until the desired amount has collected on the glass.

Measure the tequila, triple sec, and lemon or lime juice into a 16-ounce cocktail shaker glass full of ice. Place a stainless steel cocktail shaker over the glass, tapping the top to create a seal. Shake vigorously for about 5 seconds and pour into the salt-rimmed glass.

Tequila Tidbit We like the rich, natural flavor of Bols triple sec, but there are other brands on the market. If you are considering buying another brand, be sure to read the label. We recommend only investing in a triple sec that uses the natural flavors of exotic oranges and orange peel. Definitely avoid those that contain artificial flavors.

LA HERRADURA FUERTE MARGARITA

Makes 1 margarita

Fuerte *means "strong." Alcoholic spirits are measured for their strength by the "proof," which is double their percentage of alcohol. Thus, a 100-proof liquor is 50 percent alcohol (table wine is usually 12 to 14 percent alcohol). The higher the proof, the stronger the drink. Almost all tequilas, like most other alcoholic spirits, are 80 proof. Well, with that lesson under our belts, we come to the reason for naming this margarita "La Herradura Fuerte." Herradura has begun bottling a tequila called "Herradura Blanco 46," which is 92 proof, and it is indeed 15 percent stronger than most other tequilas. This, then, is the strong Herradura margarita—La Margarita Herradura Fuerte.*

> 1 lemon or lime wedge
> Saucer of kosher salt (about ¼ inch deep)
> 1¼ ounces Herradura Blanco 46 tequila
> 1 ounce Cointreau
> 1½ ounces freshly squeezed lemon or lime juice
> Ice

Run the lemon or lime wedge around the rim of a hurricane-style margarita glass. Dip the rim of the glass into the saucer of salt, rotating the rim in the salt until the desired amount has collected on the glass.

Measure the tequila, Cointreau, and lemon or lime juice into a 16-ounce cocktail shaker glass full of ice. Place a stainless steel cocktail shaker over the glass, tapping the top to create a seal. Shake vigorously for about 5 seconds and pour into the salt-rimmed glass.

Margarita Tip It is a common misconception that margaritas were invented to cool off the heat of chiles in Mexican food. Not so—in fact, a lot of Mexican food isn't hot at all. On the other hand, since most New Mexican, modern Southwestern, and Tex-Mex food is **picante**, perhaps the margarita does make a nice alternative to beer when you're eating our wonderful regional fare.

Tequila Tidbit Blue agave "leaves" are shaped rather like swords, with a sharp tip. They are called **pencas** in Mexico. These "leaves" are removed before the heart of the plant is processed to make tequila.

THE SANTIAGO MARGARITA

Makes 1 margarita

This margarita was inspired by a longtime Maria's patron named James (Santiago translates as St. James in English), who wanted to improve on an existing margarita, The Rafael (see page 36). James suggested that we substitute Herradura Silver 100 percent blue agave tequila for the Cuervo Especial, and whaddya know, he helped us create one of the smoothest and most elegant margaritas around.

> 1 lemon or lime wedge
> Saucer of kosher salt (about ¼ inch deep)
> 1¼ ounces Herradura Silver tequila
> 1 ounce Cointreau
> 1½ ounces freshly squeezed lemon or lime juice
> Ice

Run the lemon or lime wedge around the rim of a hurricane-style margarita glass. Dip the rim of the glass into the saucer of salt, rotating the rim in the salt until the desired amount has collected on the glass.

Measure the tequila, Cointreau, and lemon or lime juice into a 16-ounce cocktail shaker glass full of ice. Place a stainless steel cocktail shaker over the glass, tapping the top to create a seal. Shake vigorously for about 5 seconds and pour into the salt-rimmed glass.

Tequila Tidbit The major tequila producers each own several million agave plants, and a few grow them organically. Herradura is one of these ecologically friendly producers.

THE HERRADURA GOLD MARGARITA

Makes 1 margarita

Back when tequila in the United States was exclusive to the Southwest because the East Coast hadn't yet discovered it, tequila aficionados would brag about the smooth, outstanding flavor of Herradura Gold. These folks would never use this wonderful nectar in a margarita— "Sorry," they'd say, "this is sippin' stuff." Well, we think this "sippin' stuff" makes an awesome margarita. Herradura recently changed their label to read "Reposado" instead of "Gold" to keep up with the market of more knowledgeable consumers.

> 1 lemon or lime wedge
> Saucer of kosher salt (about ¼ inch deep)
> 1¼ ounces Herradura Reposado tequila
> 1 ounce Cointreau
> 1½ ounces freshly squeezed lemon or lime juice
> Ice

Run the lemon or lime wedge around the rim of a hurricane-style margarita glass. Dip the rim of the glass into the saucer of salt, rotating the rim in the salt until the desired amount has collected on the glass.

Measure the tequila, Cointreau, and lemon or lime juice into a 16-ounce cocktail shaker glass full of ice. Place a stainless steel cocktail shaker over the glass, tapping the top to create a seal. Shake vigorously for about 5 seconds and pour into the salt-rimmed glass.

Margarita Tip The glasses we use for our real margaritas are made by the Libbey Glass Company. The hurricane-style, 13¼-ounce "rocks" glasses are called "Poco Grande II." The saucer-type glasses are Coupette/Margarita. They can be ordered from a good kitchen store or any Libbey Glass dealer.

Tequila Tidbit The blue agave flavor of Herradura Reposado is enhanced by aging in oak barrels, which imparts a light golden hue to the tequila. Herradura Silver is a premium tequila, produced from 100 percent blue agave, with no aging.

THE HERRADURA AÑEJO MARGARITA

Makes 1 margarita

Herradura was the first 100 percent blue agave tequila to be imported into the United States and effectively marketed, which gave it a head start on other superpremium brands. This is probably the main reason why it is just about the best-known of the superpremium tequilas available; some tequila fans would say that this is the finest of them all. The rich, flavorful taste of Herradura Añejo tequila is enhanced by two full years of aging.

> 1 lemon or lime wedge
> Saucer of kosher salt (about ¼ inch deep)
> 1¼ ounces Herradura Añejo tequila
> 1 ounce Cointreau
> 1½ ounces freshly squeezed lemon or lime juice
> Ice

Run the lemon or lime wedge around the rim of a hurricane-style margarita glass. Dip the rim of the glass into the saucer of salt, rotating the rim in the salt until the desired amount has collected on the glass.

Measure the tequila, Cointreau, and lemon or lime juice into a 16-ounce cocktail shaker glass full of ice. Place a stainless steel cocktail shaker over the glass, tapping the top to create a seal. Shake vigorously for about 5 seconds and pour into the salt-rimmed glass.

Tequila Tidbit The blue agave plant is a succulent and not a cactus, as some people would have you believe. It is kin to the aloe vera plant, which it resembles on a bigger scale. (Maybe that explains why 100 percent agave tequila is so smooth!)

THE SUE "GEE!" MARGARITA

Makes 1 margarita

When longtime friend Suegy Randall was in grade school, there was another Sue in her class. Our Sue, whose maiden name was Getty, became Sue G., and the name has stuck. With a story like that, we had to name a margarita after her. So, when Herradura came along with their 100 percent agave blanco tequila called Hacienda del Cristero, we mixed it with Cointreau and thought the smooth elegance of the concoction perfectly matched Suegy's nature. And since one of our recipe testers remarked "Gee! That's good," after the first sip, we decided we had to name it for Suegy.

> 1 lemon or lime wedge
> Saucer of kosher salt (about ¼ inch deep)
> 1¼ ounces Hacienda del Cristero Blanco tequila
> 1 ounce Cointreau
> 1½ ounces freshly squeezed lemon or lime juice
> Ice

Run the lemon or lime wedge around the rim of a hurricane-style margarita glass. Dip the rim of the glass into the saucer of salt, rotating the rim in the salt until the desired amount has collected on the glass.

Measure the tequila, Cointreau, and lemon or lime juice into a 16-ounce cocktail shaker glass full of ice. Place a stainless steel cocktail shaker over the glass, tapping the top to create a seal. Shake vigorously for about 5 seconds and pour into the salt-rimmed glass.

Tequila Tidbit Most agave growers trim the maturing plants to avoid workers stabbing themselves on the sharp ends of the leaves. Some tequila makers think that agave plants that are not trimmed during the growing period result in a stronger, healthier plant. The growers that don't trim their agave need very careful workers.

Margarita Tip If you can't find freshly squeezed lemon or lime juice and you don't want to bother with squeezing the lemons or limes yourself, be sure the juice you use in your margaritas is unsweetened. Beware of frozen lemonades or limeades. They are generally packed with sugar. The best bet is still to squeeze your own.

El Tesoro

El Tesoro tequilas are arguably the finest tequilas of all. They are handmade from estate-grown agave only, and every piña is harvested when it is individually mature, rather than when most of the agave in one field or another are ready. The piñas are then cut, roasted in steam ovens for two days, and squeezed with a huge millstone to extract the sweetness. The juice is then transferred by hand to vats, fermented, then double distilled to the exact proof desired. El Tesoro is literally fermented to proof; the aguamiel, or sweet agave juice, is poured into fermenting vats with the exact amount of yeast to begin the fermentation process. It is one of the most flavorful of all tequilas because nothing else is added. All this makes El Tesoro one of the purest forms of alcoholic beverage made today.

In 2003, El Tesoro's new importer, Jim Beam, did a total repackaging of the El Tesoro Platinum (Blanco) Reposado and Añejo. The bottles are a bit more modern, but not so extravagant as to drive up the cost. They are calling their Blanco, "Platinum," rather than the normal "Silver"—don't be confused, it's still the same thing.

THE ELIZABETH II MARGARITA
Makes 1 margarita

One of Maria's cocktail waitresses, Elizabeth, was explaining to a customer that when a margarita was mixed using the premium El Tesoro tequila and Grand Marnier, the latter dominated the tequila, while a margarita made with El Tesoro and Cointreau allowed the flavor to emerge more fully. The customer was a Grand Marnier lover, however, and asked Elizabeth if the bartender would be willing to mix a margarita using El Tesoro, a half measure of Grand Marnier, and a half measure of Cointreau. It proved to be a winning combination, and the name Elizabeth II stuck, referring to one Elizabeth and two orange liqueurs. For as long as I can remember, anyone who has ordered an Elizabeth II once has ordered it again.

> 1 lemon or lime wedge
> Saucer of kosher salt (about ¼ inch deep)
> 1¼ ounces El Tesoro Platinum tequila
> ½ ounce Grand Marnier
> ½ ounce Cointreau
> 1½ ounces freshly squeezed lemon or lime juice
> Ice

Run the lemon or lime wedge around the rim of a hurricane-style margarita glass. Dip the rim of the glass into the saucer of salt, rotating the rim in the salt until the desired amount has collected on the glass.

Measure the tequila, Grand Marnier, Cointreau, and lemon or lime juice into a 16-ounce cocktail shaker glass full of ice. Place a stainless steel cocktail shaker over the glass, tapping the top to create a seal. Shake vigorously for about 5 seconds and pour into the salt-rimmed glass.

Tequila Tidbit All El Tesoro tequilas are 100 percent blue agave, handmade, and double distilled at precisely the right time to produce an 80-proof liquor (40 percent alcohol by volume). Most other distilled spirits either have distilled water added to lower the proof or alcohol added to raise the proof.

MARIA'S FAMOUS LA ULTIMA MARGARITA

Makes 1 margarita

This is one of the very first superpremium margaritas to be marketed in the world. Up until this particular margarita, most tequila connoisseurs would only drink their precious 100 percent superpremium nectar straight. There should be no substituting of any of the ingredients in this margarita. Taste them all together and I'm confident that you will find it will live up to its name, "The Ultimate Margarita."

1 lemon or lime wedge
Saucer of kosher salt (about ¼ inch deep)
1¼ ounces El Tesoro Platinum tequila
1 ounce Cointreau
1½ ounces freshly squeezed lemon or lime juice
Ice

Run the lemon or lime wedge around the rim of a hurricane-style margarita glass. Dip the rim of the glass into the saucer of salt, rotating the rim in the salt until the desired amount has collected on the glass.

Measure the tequila, Cointreau, and lemon or lime juice into a 16-ounce cocktail shaker glass full of ice. Place a stainless steel cocktail shaker over the glass, tapping the top to create a seal. Shake vigorously for about 5 seconds and pour into the salt-rimmed glass.

Margarita Tip This margarita regularly spawns debate with tequila connoisseurs who accuse us of violating the integrity of the tequila by using it in a margarita. So you be the judge. Sip a little El Tesoro Platinum on its own. Then make up this margarita and taste it. Which is more pleasant? I think the margarita is so much more enjoyable than even the best tequila. (I rarely drink tequila straight anymore.)

Tequila Tidbit Maria's pours more El Tesoro tequila than any other restaurant or bar in America. Our Maria's Famous la Ultima Margarita is largely responsible for this.

THE GRAND PLATINUM MARGARITA

Makes 1 margarita

This margarita is made with two of the most expensive distilled spirits available: 100 percent blue agave El Tesoro Platinum (silver) tequila and Grand Marnier. You do get what you pay for, though. Here is a world-class cocktail that is probably one of the purest, most natural concoctions you can enjoy. El Tesoro is handmade and double distilled to proof, while Grand Marnier is triple distilled from exotic oranges and peels with premium cognac added. And of course, the lemon juice is freshly squeezed from one of nature's most efficient and remarkable containers.

> 1 lemon or lime wedge
> Saucer of kosher salt (about ¼ inch deep)
> 1¼ ounces El Tesoro Platinum tequila
> 1 ounce Grand Marnier
> 1½ ounces freshly squeezed lemon or lime juice
> Ice

Run the lemon or lime wedge around the rim of a hurricane-style margarita glass. Dip the rim of the glass into the saucer of salt, rotating the rim in the salt until the desired amount has collected on the glass.

Measure the tequila, Grand Marnier, and lemon or lime juice into a 16-ounce cocktail shaker glass full of ice. Place a stainless steel cocktail shaker over the glass, tapping the top to create a seal. Shake vigorously for about 5 seconds and pour into the salt-rimmed glass.

Tequila Tidbit A few tequila makers still grow, harvest, cook, and distill their own agave and wouldn't think of using any other agave. One such tequila is El Tesoro de Don Felipe (we refer to this brand as simply "El Tesoro"), from the highlands of Jalisco in the Arandas area of Mexico. There, Don Felipe and his family select only the agave piñas that have reached maturity and harvest them for their estate-grown 100 percent agave tequila. The advantage: total quality control, from planting to cultivating to harvesting to distilling and bottling (not unlike estate-grown and –bottled Bordeaux in France).

THE MOONGLOW MARGARITA

Makes 1 margarita

El Tesoro de Don Felipe tequila was one of the first 100 percent agave superpremium tequilas to be imported into the United States, after the longstanding reign of Herradura, which was the first such tequila on U.S. shelves. For many years, El Tesoro was available only in blanco and añejo, and eager El Tesoro fans waited and waited for the reposado to be imported. Finally it was. We immediately mixed it with Cointreau and lemon juice and couldn't help but notice the color of the margarita was that of moonglow—hence the name. Mix it up and you'll agree.

  1 lemon or lime wedge
  Saucer of kosher salt (about ¼ inch deep)
  1¼ ounces El Tesoro Reposado tequila
  1 ounce Cointreau
  1½ ounces freshly squeezed lemon or lime juice
  Ice

Run the lemon or lime wedge around the rim of a hurricane-style margarita glass. Dip the rim of the glass into the saucer of salt, rotating the rim in the salt until the desired amount has collected on the glass.

Measure the tequila, Cointreau, and lemon or lime juice into a 16-ounce cocktail shaker glass full of ice. Place a stainless steel cocktail shaker over the glass, tapping the top to create a seal. Shake vigorously for about 5 seconds and pour into the salt-rimmed glass.

Margarita Tip Invite some friends over and compare the different flavors you are able to create by using a single tequila (such as El Tesoro) and interchanging the Cointreau with Grand Marnier or triple sec. You can also experiment with substituting fresh lime juice for the lemon juice.

Tequila Tidbit The silicate-based volcanic soil around Tequila in the state of Jalisco (which produces by far the most tequila) is ideal for growing the blue agave plant.

THE GRAND MOONGLOW MARGARITA

Makes 1 margarita

The arrival of the reposado 100 percent agave tequila from El Tesoro was such a treat and it made such a delightful visual and taste experience with the Cointreau, we had to try it with Grand Marnier. The result: Grand! The moonglow coloring was a bit deeper with the Grand Marnier, and the taste was outstanding—just a bit stronger than with the Cointreau. The hint of the cognac used in the Grand Marnier makes our Grand Moonglow a favorite at Maria's!

1 lemon or lime wedge
Saucer of kosher salt (about ¼ inch deep)
1¼ ounces El Tesoro Reposado tequila
1 ounce Grand Marnier
1½ ounces freshly squeezed lemon or lime juice
Ice

Run the lemon or lime wedge around the rim of a hurricane-style margarita glass. Dip the rim of the glass into the saucer of salt, rotating the rim in the salt until the desired amount has collected on the glass.

Measure the tequila, Grand Marnier, and lemon or lime juice into a 16-ounce cocktail shaker glass full of ice. Place a stainless steel cocktail shaker over the glass, tapping the top to create a seal. Shake vigorously for about 5 seconds and pour into the salt-rimmed glass.

Tequila Tidbit The mature blue agave plant is called the **madre** (mother plant) by tequila growers. The young plants that spring from the madre's roots are called **hijuelos**, or "little children." These offspring are left to grow next to the mother plant for 4 or 5 years before they are replanted.

EL BAILE DEL SOL MARGARITA
Makes 1 margarita

This margarita is a salute to our friend—the fellow who says all those kind things about Maria's in the foreword of this book—the Sundance Kid, Robert Redford. This exceptional margarita uses 3/4 ounce of 100 percent agave El Tesoro Añejo tequila blended with the same amount of 100 percent agave Chinaco Añejo tequila. They dance together with the sunshine of Cointreau and freshly squeezed lemon juice to create the fantastic margarita named "El Baile del Sol," which translates to "The Sundance."

1 lemon or lime wedge
Saucer of kosher salt (about 1/4 inch deep)
3/4 ounce El Tesoro Añejo tequila
3/4 ounce Chinaco Añejo tequila
1 ounce Cointreau
1 1/2 ounces freshly squeezed lemon or lime juice
Ice

Run the lemon or lime wedge around the rim of a hurricane-style margarita glass. Dip the rim of the glass into the saucer of salt, rotating the rim in the salt until the desired amount has collected on the glass.

Measure the tequilas, Cointreau, and lemon or lime juice into a 16-ounce cocktail shaker glass full of ice. Place a stainless steel cocktail shaker over the glass, tapping the top to create a seal. Shake vigorously for about 5 seconds and pour into the salt-rimmed glass.

Margarita Tip Because you are going to be the margarita maven in your circle of friends, invest in a small, 3-pound box of kosher salt. This will last awhile and is sure to really impress your pals.

Tequila Tidbit If you travel to Mexico and despair when you cannot find El Tesoro anywhere on the shelves, take heart! This family of tequilas is called Tapatio south of the border. Other tequila makers also market their products under different brand names at home and abroad.

THE GRAND TREASURE MARGARITA

Makes 1 margarita

Tequila lovers who have tried most of the 100 percent blue agave tequilas on the market generally have their own preferred sipping tequila. El Tesoro Añejo tequila is certainly a contender for the title of Best Tequila in the World (let's not pull any punches). This is a tequila to enjoy in a brandy snifter after dinner. Try it sometime—you'll think you're sipping a fine cognac. This margarita combines muy añejo tequila with Grand Marnier, which is popular with those who enjoy a heavier alcohol taste rather than the subtle agave flavor of silver tequilas.

    1 lemon or lime wedge
    Saucer of kosher salt (about ¼ inch deep)
    1¼ ounces El Tesoro Añejo tequila
    1 ounce Grand Marnier
    1½ ounces freshly squeezed lemon or lime juice
    Ice

Run the lemon or lime wedge around the rim of a hurricane-style margarita glass. Dip the rim of the glass into the saucer of salt, rotating the rim in the salt until the desired amount has collected on the glass.

Measure the tequila, Grand Marnier, and lemon or lime juice into a 16-ounce cocktail shaker glass full of ice. Place a stainless steel cocktail shaker over the glass, tapping the top to create a seal. Shake vigorously for about 5 seconds and pour into the salt-rimmed glass.

Margarita Tip At Maria's we think tequila should be drunk in margaritas, so we strongly discourage shots and slammers—we believe folks have a tendency to overindulge when drinking tequila this way. We want our guests to drink liquor because they like it, not because they want to get drunk.

Tequila Tidbit Even though the golden El Tesoro Añejo tequila is handmade, double distilled to proof, and then carefully aged in oak barrels for more than two years, I prefer the "fresh" newly distilled El Tesoro Platinum (silver). The aging process seems to cause the tequila to lose the deep agave flavor that is unique to super-premium 100 percent blue agave tequila.

LA MARGARITA DEL JOVEN ESTEBAN

Makes 1 margarita

We named this margarita after one of Maria's longtime waiters, Steve Young (joven means "young"), who couldn't understand why we didn't have a margarita on our list that combined the El Tesoro Añejo and Cointreau. After all, we had both El Tesoro Platinum and El Tesoro Añejo margaritas mixed with Cointreau. Steve conned us into believing that his customers insisted on El Tesoro Añejo and Cointreau margaritas (which they did—after a little coaching from Steve). Since we believe that the customer is always right, and because we heard rave reviews from the customers drinking this concoction, we decided to add it to our Great Margaritas List and name it after Steve.

> 1 lemon or lime wedge
> Saucer of kosher salt (about ¼ inch deep)
> 1¼ ounces El Tesoro Añejo tequila
> 1 ounce Cointreau
> 1½ ounces freshly squeezed lemon or lime juice
> Ice

Run the lemon or lime wedge around the rim of a hurricane-style margarita glass. Dip the rim of the glass into the saucer of salt, rotating the rim in the salt until the desired amount has collected on the glass.

Measure the tequila, Cointreau, and lemon or lime juice into a 16-ounce cocktail shaker glass full of ice. Place a stainless steel cocktail shaker over the glass, tapping the top to create a seal. Shake vigorously for about 5 seconds and pour into the salt-rimmed glass.

Tequila Tidbit Many tequila producers will tell you that their tequila is unique because of their water supply, and that it is the water used in the distilling process that makes all the difference to flavor and quality. Many producers boast that their own private wells produce the best water.

LA MARGARITA DE PARADISO
Makes 1 margarita

Yes, my friends, this is the $42 margarita. The first thing people ask about this drink is, "Is it really worth that much?" Our reply: "Definitely." It's made with one of the finest tequilas ever made, Paradiso by El Tesoro. The company ages freshly distilled 100 percent agave tequila in several different styles of cognac oak barrels that are imported from the Cognac region of France. Another import by El Tesoro is Alain Royer, the master cognac blender, who then weaves his magic to create the liquid nectar called Paradiso. Not wishing to stop there, we have added the 150th-anniversary Cuvée Speciale Cent Cinquantenaire Grand Marnier and lemon juice to create the most awesome margarita ever.

1 lemon or lime wedge
Saucer of kosher salt (about ¼ inch deep)
1¼ ounces El Tesoro Paradiso tequila
1 ounce Cuvée Speciale Cent Cinquantenaire Grand
   Marnier
1½ ounces freshly squeezed lemon or lime juice
Ice

Run the lemon or lime wedge around the rim of a hurricane-style margarita glass. Dip the rim of the glass into the saucer of salt, rotating the rim in the salt until the desired amount has collected on the glass.

Measure the tequila, Grand Marnier, and lemon or lime juice into a 16-ounce cocktail shaker glass full of ice. Place a stainless steel cocktail shaker over the glass, tapping the top to create a seal. Shake vigorously for about 5 seconds and pour into the salt-rimmed glass.

Tequila Tidbit The tequila and Grand Marnier used in this cocktail are very expensive, and we advise keeping them together—do not substitute either one. Paradiso served on its own in a brandy snifter will rival the finest cognac.

Patrón

Patrón is one of the great original entries into the U.S. superpremium 100 percent blue agave market. You know you're in for a treat the minute you see the unique hand-blown reusable decanter-type bottle, complete with a cork-lined handblown glass stopper. On the other hand, there's no free lunch, as they say, and though this is an outstanding tequila, Patrón is generally a little higher priced than others of comparable quality, almost certainly because of its superior packaging. If you have use for the decanter, Patrón is a particular bargain; if not, you will be paying for it anyway—you be the judge.

THE DON ROBERTO MARGARITA

Makes 1 margarita

This margarita is named for Bob Noyes, a former partner of ours at Maria's, both because he is a patrón—*one of the bosses—and because this is his favorite margarita. It features Patrón Añejo tequila, which like the silver version (page 76) is bottled in handblown glass decanter-type bottles.*

> 1 lemon or lime wedge
> Saucer of kosher salt (about ¼ inch deep)
> 1¼ ounces Patrón Añejo tequila
> 1 ounce Cointreau
> 1½ ounces freshly squeezed lemon or lime juice
> Ice

Run the lemon or lime wedge around the rim of a hurricane-style margarita glass. Dip the rim of the glass into the saucer of salt, rotating the rim in the salt until the desired amount has collected on the glass.

Measure the tequila, Cointreau, and lemon or lime juice into a 16-ounce cocktail shaker glass full of ice. Place a stainless steel cocktail shaker over the glass, tapping the top to create a seal. Shake vigorously for about 5 seconds and pour into the salt-rimmed glass.

Margarita Tip Since the word "tequila" refers to the town situated in the volcanic lava hills of the Jalisco region, we decided to experiment with a Volcano Margarita, made with dry ice (to create the volcano smoke) and Tabasco (for the heat). All the other ingredients—tequila, triple sec, and lemon juice—were as usual. It was awful. The moral of this tale is that you can experiment all you want, but not everything you try to make into a margarita is going to be a true delight.

Tequila Tidbit Blue agave plants grown for making tequila are planted about 3 feet apart, in rows. The mature plants reach 6 to 8 feet tall.

LA MARGARITA DE LA DOÑA HELEN
Makes 1 margarita

When a tequila as popular as Patrón introduces a new product, it's an exciting event for a barkeep who offers over a hundred different margaritas. That was the case when Patrón began importing its 100 percent agave reposado. With several margaritas already on the list made with Patrón Silver and Añejo tequilas, we quickly began the mixing and tasting (tough job, but somebody has to do it). The resulting margarita using Patrón Reposado and Cointreau was so smooth and elegant that we decided to name it in honor of the employee who has been with Maria's almost thirty years, Helen Maestas. Want an extrasmooth margarita? Try this one!

1 lemon or lime wedge
Saucer of kosher salt (about ¼ inch deep)
1¼ ounces Patrón Reposado tequila
1 ounce Cointreau
1½ ounces freshly squeezed lemon or lime juice
Ice

Run the lemon or lime wedge around the rim of a hurricane-style margarita glass. Dip the rim of the glass into the saucer of salt, rotating the rim in the salt until the desired amount has collected on the glass.

Measure the tequila, Cointreau, and lemon or lime juice into a 16-ounce cocktail shaker glass full of ice. Place a stainless steel cocktail shaker over the glass, tapping the top to create a seal. Shake vigorously for about 5 seconds and pour into the salt-rimmed glass.

Tequila Tidbit All Patrón tequila is made with large stone milling wheels that squeeze all the juices from the steam-cooked agave piñas. The fermentation process includes the pressed piña fibers, which the manufacturer claims help impart the unique flavor and smoothness. The fermented liquid is then double distilled and hand bottled. The quality of this particular tequila as well as the unique packaging make this one of our favorite gifts for housewarmings, holidays, or just special friends.

THE GRAND LORENZO MARGARITA
Makes 1 margarita

This margarita is named after the man who has probably hand shaken and served more margaritas from scratch than any other person on the face of the earth, Larry Felton, one of Maria's ace bartenders. This excellent margarita uses 100 percent agave Patrón Reposado tequila and Cointreau. Actually, the real tequila brand name is not just Patrón, it's Del Patrón, which means "from the boss." And Larry is the boss when it comes to making margaritas! The one-of-a-kind, handblown bottles used in Patrón tequilas are creations unto themselves. This now-familiar, square decanter bottle is worth the extra money you pay for this tequila.

> 1 lemon or lime wedge
> Saucer of kosher salt (about ¼ inch deep)
> 1¼ ounces Patrón Reposado tequila
> 1 ounce Cointreau
> 1½ ounces freshly squeezed lemon or lime juice
> Ice

Run the lemon or lime wedge around the rim of a hurricane-style margarita glass. Dip the rim of the glass into the saucer of salt, rotating the rim in the salt until the desired amount has collected on the glass.

Measure the tequila, Cointreau, and lemon or lime juice into a 16-ounce cocktail shaker glass full of ice. Place a stainless steel cocktail shaker over the glass, tapping the top to create a seal. Shake vigorously for about 5 seconds and pour into the salt-rimmed glass.

Tequila Tidbit **Although by the Mexican government's legal definition, tequila can be made in any 1 of 5 states, over 95 percent of all tequila is distilled in the state of Jalisco.**

LA MARGARITA DE LA PATRÓNA
Makes 1 margarita

This margarita is made with Patrón Silver—a 100 percent blue agave tequila from the highlands of Jalisco (an area that is increasingly touted by tequila experts as the prime agave-growing region of Mexico). Patrón in Spanish means "boss," and patróna is the feminine version, or loosely translated, "boss lady"—so here we present "the boss lady's margarita."

1 lemon or lime wedge
Saucer of kosher salt (about ¼ inch deep)
1¼ ounces Patrón Silver tequila
1 ounce Cointreau
1½ ounces freshly squeezed lemon or lime juice
Ice

Run the lemon or lime wedge around the rim of a hurricane-style margarita glass. Dip the rim of the glass into the saucer of salt, rotating the rim in the salt until the desired amount has collected on the glass.

Measure the tequila, Cointreau, and lemon or lime juice into a 16-ounce cocktail shaker glass full of ice. Place a stainless steel cocktail shaker over the glass, tapping the top to create a seal. Shake vigorously for about 5 seconds and pour into the salt-rimmed glass.

Tequila Tidbit By the year 2000, tequila was one of the top ten best-selling spirits in America, behind the market leader, vodka, which sells twice the volume of second place rum. In overall sales, tequila has over-taken scotch and is about to displace gin, with which it is virtually tied (both tequila and gin still trail Canadian whiskey and bourbon sales). Although the tequila market's growth has slowed, its phenomenal acceptance has given it first-class status in the spirits world and it is expected to become one of the top five best-selling liquors in America.

THE BRASS MONKEY MARGARITA
Makes 1 margarita

From the makers of Patrón comes (at last) an affordable, everyday tequila, Mico Gold. Mico Gold is a mixto; the stepsister to the very popular 100 percent agave Patrón tequila. There is no fancy bottle, but you can rely on the Patrón name to bring you a quality product. We mix Mico Gold with Bols triple sec to come up with the Brass Monkey Margarita.

1 lemon or lime wedge
Saucer of kosher salt (about ¼ inch deep)
1¼ ounces Mico Gold tequila
1 ounce Bols triple sec
1½ ounces freshly squeezed lemon or lime juice
Ice

Run the lemon or lime wedge around the rim of a hurricane-style margarita glass. Dip the rim of the glass into the saucer of salt, rotating the rim in the salt until the desired amount has collected on the glass.

Measure the tequila, triple sec, and lemon or lime juice into a 16-ounce cocktail shaker glass full of ice. Place a stainless steel cocktail shaker over the glass, tapping the top to create a seal. Shake vigorously for about 5 seconds and pour into the salt-rimmed glass.

Tequila Tidbit Mezcal is not tequila. We can call mezcal a cousin to tequila because it is generally made from the same agave plant. However, mezcal is not usually double distilled and, unlike tequila, is not subject to any governmental regulations.

THE MICO DE PLATA MARGARITA
Makes 1 margarita

Patrón, one of the most successful tequila importers and marketers, has finally developed a low-cost mixto called Mico (monkey) that comes in both silver and gold. A mixto must be at least 51 percent agave, and when you deal with a reputable tequila maker like Patrón, you know it's going to be good quality. The Mico bottle is nice, but mass-produced, thus making the cost very affordable.

> 1 lemon or lime wedge
> Saucer of kosher salt (about ¼ inch deep)
> 1¼ ounces Mico Silver tequila
> 1 ounce Bols triple sec
> 1½ ounces freshly squeezed lemon or lime juice
> Ice

Run the lemon or lime wedge around the rim of a hurricane-style margarita glass. Dip the rim of the glass into the saucer of salt, rotating the rim in the salt until the desired amount has collected on the glass.

Measure the tequila, triple sec, and lemon or lime juice into a 16-ounce cocktail shaker glass full of ice. Place a stainless steel cocktail shaker over the glass, tapping the top to create a seal. Shake vigorously for about 5 seconds and pour into the salt-rimmed glass.

Tequila Tidbit Some distillers will manufacture tequila for more than one importer. The one producer can sell his tequila to as many "brands" as he likes or as many as the traffic will bear. However, the producer's NOM number will remain the same on all the brands he produces.

Don Julio

Don Julio has been a popular premium tequila in Mexico for quite some time. Many of our Maria's customers would come in asking for Don Julio tequila after a trip to Mexico and we didn't have it. After pressuring our supplier to bring it in, it became a best seller. At first we were only able to acquire Don Julio Silver and Añejo. Fortunately, Don Julio Reposado is now a regular import and we feature it on our list as well. This is an extraordinary and reasonably priced 100 percent agave tequila.

THE DON JULIO DE ORO MARGARITA

Makes 1 margarita

It seemed like it took forever for Don Julio to be imported into the state of New Mexico. We were getting constant requests at Maria's for Don Julio from out-of-state folks, especially those from California. Our distributor kept telling us that it would be available in "the next few months." Well, finally, in early 1998, we got our first shipment of Don Julio, and the wait was definitely worth it. The 100 percent agave Don Julio Añejo tequila has tones of pepper and oak that settle on the back of the mouth. This is one of the better margaritas you'll ever shake up and serve!

1 lemon or lime wedge
Saucer of kosher salt (about ¼ inch deep)
1¼ ounces Don Julio Añejo tequila
1 ounce Cointreau
1½ ounces freshly squeezed lemon or lime juice
Ice

Run the lemon or lime wedge around the rim of a hurricane-style margarita glass. Dip the rim of the glass into the saucer of salt, rotating the rim in the salt until the desired amount has collected on the glass.

Measure the tequila, Cointreau, and lemon or lime juice into a 16-ounce cocktail shaker glass full of ice. Place a stainless steel cocktail shaker over the glass, tapping the top to create a seal. Shake vigorously for about 5 seconds and pour into the salt-rimmed glass.

Tequila Tidbit The Mexican government introduced strict rules regarding the production of tequila in the 1970s for the purpose of ensuring quality standards. These rules, enshrined in law, are called "La Norma," or the Norm, the law.

EL GRAN JULIO RESERVA MARGARITA

Makes 1 margarita

For Maria's to use Grand Marnier in a margarita, we have to make sure that the strength of the Grand Marnier does not overwhelm the flavor of the tequila, using the tried-and-true proportions in our recipes. (We could add more tequila, but it would irresponsibly increase the alcohol intake by our customers; our aim is not to get anyone drunk, but rather to serve enjoyable margaritas with our great New Mexican food.) When we tested Don Julio Añejo with Grand Marnier, not only did it hold up to the challenge of the liqueur, but the oak and pepper tones of this wonderful añejo came through like a champ.

> 1 lemon or lime wedge
> Saucer of kosher salt (about ¼ inch deep)
> 1¼ ounces Don Julio Añejo tequila
> 1 ounce Grand Marnier
> 1½ ounces freshly squeezed lemon or lime juice
> Ice

Run the lemon or lime wedge around the rim of a hurricane-style margarita glass. Dip the rim of the glass into the saucer of salt, rotating the rim in the salt until the desired amount has collected on the glass.

Measure the tequila, Grand Marnier, and lemon or lime juice into a 16-ounce cocktail shaker glass full of ice. Place a stainless steel cocktail shaker over the glass, tapping the top to create a seal. Shake vigorously for about 5 seconds and pour into the salt-rimmed glass.

Margarita Tip It can be fun to experiment with tequilas and other fruit-based liqueurs or juices—for example, a melon margarita made with tequila, Midori, and lemon juice; a watermelon margarita using watermelon juice instead of lemon juice; an apple margarita made with apple juice. Use cranberry juice, mango nectar—there's no limit. See the next chapter for some recipes.

Tequila Tidbit About 2,000 blue agave plants are grown per acre in tequila country, in neat, symmetrical rows.

THE DON JULIO PLATA MARGARITA
Makes 1 margarita

Of all the brands of tequilas that we now have on our list, the one that was re-quested most often but was missing until 1998 (when the distrib-utor finally was able to bring it into the state of New Mexico) was Don Julio. The requests were well warranted—Don Julio is a wonderful tequila and it makes a fantastic margarita. When we mixed the Don Julio Blanco with Cointreau, we were absolutely delighted with the results. The fresh aroma of the agave emerges from the drink, and once the cool liquid hits the palate, you know you've got as good a tequila as you've ever tasted.

> 1 lemon or lime wedge
> Saucer of kosher salt (about ¼ inch deep)
> 1¼ ounces Don Julio Blanco tequila
> 1 ounce Cointreau
> 1½ ounces freshly squeezed lemon or lime juice
> Ice

Run the lemon or lime wedge around the rim of a hurricane-style margarita glass. Dip the rim of the glass into the saucer of salt, rotating the rim in the salt until the desired amount has collected on the glass.

Measure the tequila, Cointreau, and lemon or lime juice into a 16-ounce cocktail shaker glass full of ice. Place a stain-less steel cocktail shaker over the glass, tapping the top to create a seal. Shake vigorously for about 5 seconds and pour into the salt-rimmed glass.

Margarita Tip In Spanish, the word **margarita** means "daisy." If you know anyone named Margarita, you can call her Daisy just to show off your phenomenal knowledge, but forget about going into a bar and ordering a "Daisy." They will only think you're strange (and bartenders don't take well to strange folk), and you'll never get your margarita!

Tequila Tidbit The word "tequila" is taken from the ancient Nahuatl (Aztec) language; it means "volcano." The village of Tequila is indeed set in the volcanic Sierra Madre.

THE GOLDHAMER MARGARITA

Makes 1 margarita

Named for our good friends Roger and Jill Goldhamer, this margarita is made with 100 percent agave Don Julio Resposado tequila and Cointreau. It tastes so good—and goes down so easy—be careful, you could get hammered! Don Julio Reposado tequila is one of the most popular super-premium tequilas sold in Mexico. We began featuring superpremium mar-garitas at Maria's in 1990 and since then, of all the tequilas we didn't have, Don Julio was the second-most-requested tequila (behind Chinaco) by people who had visited Mexico. We were thrilled when we were finally able to add Don Julio to our inventory. It is a fitting tribute to Roger and Jill to name this great margarita after them.

> 1 lemon or lime wedge
> Saucer of kosher salt (about ¼ inch deep)
> 1¼ ounces Don Julio Reposado tequila
> 1 ounce Cointreau
> 1½ ounces freshly squeezed lemon or lime juice
> Ice

Run the lemon or lime wedge around the rim of a hurricane-style margarita glass. Dip the rim of the glass into the saucer of salt, rotating the rim in the salt until the desired amount has collected on the glass.

Measure the tequila, Cointreau, and lemon or lime juice into a 16-ounce cocktail shaker glass full of ice. Place a stain-less steel cocktail shaker over the glass, tapping the top to create a seal. Shake vigorously for about 5 seconds and pour into the salt-rimmed glass.

Tequila Tidbit There is a wide variety in tech-nique and technology when it comes to produc-ing tequila. The larger producers, such as Cuervo and Sauza, use state-of-the-art technology, but the small "artisan" tequilas are handcrafted.

Other Tequilas and Margaritas

Maria's maintains a tequila list of about a hundred real tequilas. We offer over one hundred real margaritas. All of our tequilas are "real" tequilas—only a half dozen are not 100 percent agave.

Are you ready for this? Mexico is producing tequila (not all of which is 100 percent agave) under 348 different labels. Most of these tequilas are not being imported into the United States at the present time, and a lot of them are in very limited production.

Recently, in an attempt to improve the quality of all tequilas with less than 100 percent agave, the Mexican government tried to pass the requirement that all tequila be at least 60 percent agave to be considered a tequila. This attempt failed, as it was pointed out that the agave is in short supply; and since it takes so long for it to mature, it would be foolish to change something so well established, especially when it would only create more supply problems. Remember: there are only five states in Mexico in which the agave used for tequila can be grown—watch for this to change in the near future; other growing areas are bound to be added to the list because of the demand for tequila. On the other hand, however, it is said that there are so many new 100 percent agave tequilas being produced because the agave sugars are less expensive than cane sugar.

Here are recipes for margaritas made with some of the new brands that have recently found their way into the American market.

EL GRAN CENTENARIO MARGARITA

Makes 1 margarita

When the leading producer of tequila in the world decides to get into the superpremium 100 percent agave tequila game, it is already a couple of centuries ahead of the rest of the superpremium producers. That's why it was such a pleasure to see José Cuervo begin production of their Gran Centenario line. How can we put this? If Michael Jordan knows how to play basketball, José Cuervo knows how to make tequila. Cuervo is not making a big deal out of the fact that they are the makers of this tequila; they want it to succeed on its own merits. Try all three styles of Gran Centenario. This recipe calls for the reposado.

> 1 lemon or lime wedge
> Saucer of kosher salt (about ¼ inch deep)
> 1¼ ounces Gran Centenario Reposado tequila
> 1 ounce Cointreau
> 1½ ounces freshly squeezed lemon or lime juice
> Ice

Run the lemon or lime wedge around the rim of a hurricane-style margarita glass. Dip the rim of the glass into the saucer of salt, rotating the rim in the salt until the desired amount has collected on the glass.

Measure the tequila, Cointreau, and lemon or lime juice into a 16-ounce cocktail shaker glass full of ice. Place a stainless steel cocktail shaker over the glass, tapping the top to create a seal. Shake vigorously for about 5 seconds and pour into the salt-rimmed glass.

Margarita Tip If fresh lemons or limes are not available for squeezing, we suggest you use the commercially bottled Realemon, which is available in most grocery stores. Realemon is pure lemon juice with a small amount of preservative added; however, once opened, its shelf life is limited—2 or 3 days in the refrigerator at most—so be prepared to use it up or throw the rest away.

Tequila Tidbit In 1995, the Mexican government planned to raise the minimum amount of agave in tequila from 51 percent to 60 percent. However, for a number of reasons, these plans were never implemented.

EL GUSANO MARGARITA
Makes 1 margarita

You're going to have more fun with the bottle on this one than you are with the margarita. Don't be confused—a bottle of real tequila will never have a worm inside, but in this case, a worm can have a real tequila inside! This bottle from the Casta family of tequilas is in the shape of the cutest worm you've seen in a long time. The stopper is the head of the worm, complete with eyes, nose, and antennae, and the body consists of the handblown glass bottle, complete with feet and a horizontal tail. Perhaps the surprising thing is that this tequila is getting rave reviews from tequila aficionados—it's an excellent 100 percent agave reposado tequila. Because of the unusual bottle, you'll pay a bit extra for this reposado, but be warned: your guests will want the bottle!

> 1 lemon or lime wedge
> Saucer of kosher salt (about ¼ inch deep)
> 1¼ ounces Casta Gusano Real Reposado tequila
> 1 ounce Cointreau
> 1½ ounces freshly squeezed lemon or lime juice
> Ice

Run the lemon or lime wedge around the rim of a hurricane-style margarita glass. Dip the rim of the glass into the saucer of salt, rotating the rim in the salt until the desired amount has collected on the glass.

Measure the tequila, Cointreau, and lemon or lime juice into a 16-ounce cocktail shaker glass full of ice. Place a stainless steel cocktail shaker over the glass, tapping the top to create a seal. Shake vigorously for about 5 seconds and pour into the salt-rimmed glass.

Margarita Tip As in any culture, in Mexico there are all kinds of toasts to make when enjoying a drink with friends. Some toasts are simply translations from one language to another. The most common toast in the Spanish language is **Salud** (which, accompanied with the lifting of a margarita glass, means "to your health").

Tequila Tidbit Tequila bottles never, ever, contain a worm (actually a moth larva). Instead, the worm can be found in some brands of mezcal.

THE MARGARITA EL JIMADOR
Makes 1 margarita

El Jimador is wonderful 100 percent agave tequila that comes in a stan-
dard liquor bottle rather than a handblown objet d'art, so you pay for
the juice, not the decanter. We use the El Jimador Reposado tequila for
this margarita, combining it with Cointreau and our ever-present freshly
squeezed lemon juice. The reposado has a deep golden hue naturally
acquired from its rest in oak barrels for at least ninety days. The flavor
is full of agave with a mellow spicy finish, so it combines with the
oranges in the Cointreau and the pure lemon juice to make a very
respectable margarita at a reasonable price.

    1 lemon or lime wedge
    Saucer of kosher salt (about ¼ inch deep)
    1¼ ounces El Jimador Reposado tequila
    1 ounce Cointreau
    1½ ounces freshly squeezed lemon or lime juice
    Ice

Run the lemon or lime wedge around the rim of a hurricane-
style margarita glass. Dip the rim of the glass into the saucer
of salt, rotating the rim in the salt until the desired amount
has collected on the glass.

Measure the tequila, Cointreau, and lemon or lime juice
into a 16-ounce cocktail shaker glass full of ice. Place a stainless steel cocktail shaker over the glass, tapping the top to
create a seal. Shake vigorously for about 5 seconds and pour
into the salt-rimmed glass.

Tequila Tidbit By law, all tequila must be distilled
twice. The product of the first distillation is referred to as
ordinario. The second distillation brings the tequila to its
final proof, which, if over 80, must be diluted down
with water.

Margarita Tip If you plan to store any leftover
margaritas, whether it's a half a glass or a half a
punch bowl, be sure you remove any ice still unmelted.
Otherwise, the margarita will be very watery the
next day. A good margarita should keep for a couple
of days under refrigeration.

MARGARITA EL CABO WABO KEVIN
Makes 1 margarita

This tequila is a 100 percent agave reposado from Sammy Hagar's Club Cabo Wabo in the Baja. Sammy claims this tequila was a favorite of the Rolling Stones. We have used our own recipe to make a margarita that is a little bit crazy. That's why we call it the Cabo Wabo Kevin. You see, Kevin is a longtime waiter at Maria's in Santa Fe, and he is a little on the wabo-wabo side, if you get my drift. Kevin is an entertainer. He is the only person I know that can carry margaritas "two up" on the upturned palm of his hand without spilling. Kevin is a great guy, and his margarita is a great cocktail.

> 1 lemon or lime wedge
> Saucer of kosher salt (about ¼ inch deep)
> 1¼ ounces Cabo Wabo Reposado tequila
> 1 ounce Cointreau
> 1½ ounces freshly squeezed lemon or lime juice
> Ice

Run the lemon or lime wedge around the rim of a hurricane-style margarita glass. Dip the rim of the glass into the saucer of salt, rotating the rim in the salt until the desired amount has collected on the glass.

Measure the tequila, Cointreau, and lemon or lime juice into a 16-ounce cocktail shaker glass full of ice. Place a stainless steel cocktail shaker over the glass, tapping the top to create a seal. Shake vigorously for about 5 seconds and pour into the salt-rimmed glass.

Tequila Tidbit As consumers, we must be aware that some of the very fancy mouthblown bottles add to the cost of the tequila. Make sure you're paying for the tequila and not just a pretty bottle. Cabo Wabo tequila is a good example of a great tequila in a collectible bottle at a fair price.

Margarita Tip Rocker Sammy Hagar serves the Cabo Waborita at his nightclub in Cabo San Lucas. This is the recipe: In a shaker over crushed ice, squeeze 2 fresh limes. Double that with Cointreau. Double that with Cabo Wabo tequila. Add a splash of Grand Marnier. For color, add a splash of blue Curaçao. Shake and pour straight up into frozen salt-rimmed glasses. Makes 2 Cabo Waboritas.

THE DANDY RANDY RANDY

Makes 1 margarita

This margarita features a tequila that comes in the tallest spirits bottle that I have ever seen, and the flavor is even taller. The Dandy Randy Randy uses 100 percent agave Corralejo Añejo tequila and Cointreau. It's named for one of our best longtime employees, Randy Martinez.

> 1 lemon or lime wedge
> Saucer of kosher salt (about ¼ inch deep)
> 1¼ ounces Corralejo Añejo tequila
> 1 ounce Cointreau
> 1½ ounces freshly squeezed lemon or lime juice
> Ice

Run the lemon or lime wedge around the rim of a hurricane-style margarita glass. Dip the rim of the glass into the saucer of salt, rotating the rim in the salt until the desired amount has collected on the glass.

Measure the tequila, Cointreau, and lemon or lime juice into a 16-ounce cocktail shaker glass full of ice. Place a stainless steel cocktail shaker over the glass, tapping the top to create a seal. Shake vigorously for about 5 seconds and pour into the salt-rimmed glass.

Tequila Tidbit Nearly 100 percent of all oak barrels used to age tequila are used whiskey barrels from whiskey makers in Kentucky (and other regions). Most often they are scraped or at least scrubbed before being used for tequila.

Margarita Tip Take this tip from the folks at Maria's: Experiment with different combinations of tequilas and Cointreau, triple sec, or Grand Marnier. Simply follow one of our margarita recipes, replacing the tequila and triple sec with your own ingredients. Once you've come up with the perfect combination, have friends over and name it after your best pal.

THE HAGAR'S REVENGE MARGARITA

Makes 1 margarita

Here is Sammy Hagar's 100 percent agave Cabo Wabo Añejo tequila mixed with Cointreau, and like it says on our Great Margarita List at Maria's, the revenge is for those who didn't buy Sammy's last CD (because this margarita costs more than his last CD!). It's a toss-up as to whether you will like the margarita or the CD best. The tequila is from the region of Jalisco and has been aged on oak for at least one year. All kidding aside, this is really an elegant margarita and the best part is that if you don't like this margarita, you will enjoy sipping the Cabo Wabo Añejo on its own!

> 1 lemon or lime wedge
> Saucer of kosher salt (about 1/4 inch deep)
> 1 1/4 ounces Cabo Wabo Añejo tequila
> 1 ounce Cointreau
> 1 1/2 ounces freshly squeezed lemon or lime juice
> Ice

Run the lemon or lime wedge around the rim of a hurricane-style margarita glass. Dip the rim of the glass into the saucer of salt, rotating the rim in the salt until the desired amount has collected on the glass.

Measure the tequila, Cointreau, and lemon or lime juice into a 16-ounce cocktail shaker glass full of ice. Place a stainless steel cocktail shaker over the glass, tapping the top to create a seal. Shake vigorously for about 5 seconds and pour into the salt-rimmed glass.

Tequila Tidbit While tequila is made exclusively from the blue agave, other agaves are processed to make alcoholic beverages. In addition to mezcal, **bacanora** is produced in the northern state of Sonora, **raicilla** is produced in Jalisco, and **comiteca** is another regional variation on the same theme. With the exception of mezcal, these local liquors are only found in Mexico and are not exported.

LA MARGARITA CAZADORES

Makes 1 margarita

I have been reading about Cazadores tequila for many years and was impressed by their distillery in Arandas, Jalisco. This tequila has only recently been imported into the United States and it is one of the best buys in a 100 percent agave reposado. Cazadores has been a favorite among the folks who live in Mexico for many years, most likely because it's a quality product and it is reasonably priced. For this margarita we have mixed Cazadores with Cointreau to come up with a mellow, dry, and great-tasting margarita.

> 1 lemon or lime wedge
> Saucer of kosher salt (about ¼ inch deep)
> 1¼ ounces Cazadores Reposado tequila
> 1 ounce Cointreau
> 1½ ounces freshly squeezed lemon or lime juice
> Ice

Run the lemon or lime wedge around the rim of a hurricane-style margarita glass. Dip the rim of the glass into the saucer of salt, rotating the rim in the salt until the desired amount has collected on the glass.

Measure the tequila, Cointreau, and lemon or lime juice into a 16-ounce cocktail shaker glass full of ice. Place a stainless steel cocktail shaker over the glass, tapping the top to create a seal. Shake vigorously for about 5 seconds and pour into the salt-rimmed glass.

Tequila Tidbit There are dozens of new tequilas entering the U.S. market annually. Most of the new tequilas are 100 percent agave and are brought in by new American importers trying to create a niche in the tequila market with clever names and/or packaging. Remember, it has to say, "bottled in Mexico" or "estate bottled at the distillery" for it to be 100 percent agave.

Margarita Tip As long as you have tequila and Cointreau, triple sec, or Grand Marnier among your list of ingredients, it should be considered a margarita, regardless of the fruit or fruit juice you use in place of the lemon. If you use some other fruit, be sure it's ripe. You should generally blend it with ice.

HUSSONG'S SPECIAL MARGARITA
Makes 1 margarita

According to the label, "Juan Hussong built the cantina (Hussong's in Ensenada, Mexico) in 1892 to accommodate fortune-seeking stagecoach riders. The cantina has since become a mecca for travelers from around the world who come to seek good times and good friends. In their search they discover still another treasure—a rare tequila that for many years was a well-hidden secret."

At Hussong's cantina, the margaritas are made by mixing equal parts of Hussong's tequila, Cointreau, and lemon juice, and served over ice in a salt-rimmed glass.

> 1 lemon or lime wedge
> Saucer of kosher salt (about ¼ inch deep)
> 1¼ ounces Hussong's Reposado tequila
> 1 ounce Cointreau
> 1½ ounces freshly squeezed lemon or lime juice
> Ice

Run the lemon or lime wedge around the rim of a hurricane-style margarita glass. Dip the rim of the glass into the saucer of salt, rotating the rim in the salt until the desired amount has collected on the glass.

Measure the tequila, Cointreau, and lemon or lime juice into a 16-ounce cocktail shaker glass full of ice. Place a stainless steel cocktail shaker over the glass, tapping the top to create a seal. Shake vigorously for about 5 seconds and pour into the salt-rimmed glass.

Tequila Tidbit The golden hue found in most aged tequilas (reposado, añejo, and muy añejo) comes from the oaken barrels in which the original white tequila is placed. The more aging the tequila has does not necessarily mean the darker gold it will be. The intensity of the color is dependent on both the duration of the aging process and the type of oak barrel that is used.

LA MARGARITA DE LOS DOS ANGELES

Makes 1 margarita

This margarita is named after two guys named Engles (engles is German for "angels"). Los dos angeles means "the two angels," but neither of these guys are! They are friends of Maria's, and we just had to name a margarita after them. This margarita uses El Jimador 100 percent agave silver tequila, a moderately priced tequila and a quite good value. We mix it with Cointreau and freshly squeezed lemon juice to create the "Two Angels Margarita." Mix one up and see if you don't agree that, despite its name, this margarita is a bit on the devilish side.

    1 lemon or lime wedge
    Saucer of kosher salt (about ¼ inch deep)
    1¼ ounces El Jimador Silver tequila
    1 ounce Cointreau
    1½ ounces freshly squeezed lemon or lime juice
    Ice

Run the lemon or lime wedge around the rim of a hurricane-style margarita glass. Dip the rim of the glass into the saucer of salt, rotating the rim in the salt until the desired amount has collected on the glass.

Measure the tequila, Cointreau, and lemon or lime juice into a 16-ounce cocktail shaker glass full of ice. Place a stainless steel cocktail shaker over the glass, tapping the top to create a seal. Shake vigorously for about 5 seconds and pour into the salt-rimmed glass.

Tequila Tidbit We are sometimes asked if the rumor that tequila is an aphrodisiac is true. Well, we like to think it is, but alas, there is no scientific evidence (yet) to support our wishful thinking.

LA MARGARITA DEL DUEÑO
Makes 1 margarita

One thinks of a fine wine when referring to a beverage as "Reserva del Dueño" (Proprietor's Reserve). But when you taste this tequila, you understand what the distiller is trying to convey with the name; it's a prestigious description that applies equally well to this tequila. This is indeed the good stuff—the stuff that the owner or proprietor has held back for himself and his nearest and dearest! In this recipe, Reserva del Dueño is mixed with Cointreau and freshly squeezed lemon juice to make a margarita that could just as easily be called "The Proprietor's Reserve."

1 lemon or lime wedge
Saucer of kosher salt (about ¼ inch deep)
1¼ ounces Reserva del Dueño tequila
1 ounce Cointreau
1½ ounces freshly squeezed lemon or lime juice
Ice

Run the lemon or lime wedge around the rim of a hurricane-style margarita glass. Dip the rim of the glass into the saucer of salt, rotating the rim in the salt until the desired amount has collected on the glass.

Measure the tequila, Cointreau, and lemon or lime juice into a 16-ounce cocktail shaker glass full of ice. Place a stainless steel cocktail shaker over the glass, tapping the top to create a seal. Shake vigorously for about 5 seconds and pour into the salt-rimmed glass.

Margarita Tip Here's another toast offered in Mexico (imported from Spain); that's a little more elaborate than the simple "Salud": Salud, dinero, y amor, y tiempo para gustarlos. ("Health, money, and love, and the time to enjoy them.")

Tequila Tidbit The amount and duration of heat during the fermentation process does affect the flavor and quality of the finished tequila. If the process takes a long time, and the mixture is not overheated, then it is more likely that the delicate flavors of the agave will show through.

THE BOOGIE WOOGIE
Makes 1 margarita

The Boogie Woogie is made from a new entry in the 100 percent agave tequila imports, Chamucos. Actually, chamuco means "bogeyman" in Spanish, but margaritas are too much fun to introduce any kind of a negative as a name for one, so we went with the Boogie Woogie. After all there can't be much more fun than doing the boogie woogie—that is, until you've tried this margarita. Chamucos is a 100 percent agave reposado tequila marketed in a tall bottle with a label that has all kinds of spirits and bogeymen on it. Don't let the label scare you away . . . it's a great tequila.

> 1 lemon or lime wedge
> Saucer of kosher salt (about ¼ inch deep)
> 1¼ ounces Chamucos Reposado Especial tequila
> 1 ounce Cointreau
> 1½ ounces freshly squeezed lemon or lime juice
> Ice

Run the lemon or lime wedge around the rim of a hurricane-style margarita glass. Dip the rim of the glass into the saucer of salt, rotating the rim in the salt until the desired amount has collected on the glass.

Measure the tequila, Cointreau, and lemon or lime juice into a 16-ounce cocktail shaker glass full of ice. Place a stainless steel cocktail shaker over the glass, tapping the top to create a seal. Shake vigorously for about 5 seconds and pour into the salt-rimmed glass.

Tequila Tidbit The blue agave used to make tequila is selected for its concentrated sugar content (A.R.T.). Industry standards are 20 percent minimum sugar concentrated agave. Most distillers try to exceed 25 percent A.R.T. agave. This allows for higher standards in quality and a more efficient fermentation and distillation.

Margarita Tip There is now a wide selection of colored salts specifically packaged for making margaritas. These should be available at your favorite bar- or kitchen-supply store. If you can't find them on your dealer's shelves, simply ask the proprietor to order them for you.

LA HACIENDA CORRALEJO MARGARITA
Makes 1 margarita

This margarita is made with 100 percent agave Corralejo Reposado tequila. The bottle is handblown glass and stands nearly 2 feet tall. The label claims that the Hacienda Corralejo was established in 1755. I think this is the date of the hacienda, not the first production of tequila. Corralejo has the first label with a health warning in Spanish on it: "El abuso en el consumo de este producto es nocivo para la salud," which means, "The abuse in the consumption of this product is harmful to your health." This is great tequila, and in blind margarita tastings, it won the hearts of many of Maria's faithful. Mix it with Cointreau and enjoy.

1 lemon or lime wedge
Saucer of kosher salt (about ¼ inch deep)
1¼ ounces Corralejo Reposado tequila
1 ounce Cointreau
1½ ounces freshly squeezed lemon or lime juice
Ice

Run the lemon or lime wedge around the rim of a hurricane-style margarita glass. Dip the rim of the glass into the saucer of salt, rotating the rim in the salt until the desired amount has collected on the glass.

Measure the tequila, Cointreau, and lemon or lime juice into a 16-ounce cocktail shaker glass full of ice. Place a stainless steel cocktail shaker over the glass, tapping the top to create a seal. Shake vigorously for about 5 seconds and pour into the salt-rimmed glass.

Tequila Tidbit The Zapotec and Mixtec Indians in the Oaxaca area would ferment the sap taken from the roots, stalks, and leaves of wild agave plants to create a drink now called **pulque**. Indians of Mexico still use pulque as a major home remedy. Medicinal herbs are often mixed with pulque to increase their benefit.

Margarita Tip Encourage your guests to enjoy their margaritas directly from the salt-rimmed glass, rather than through a straw. At Maria's we serve our margaritas with a straw, but it is only to be used as a stirrer. The salt creates a completely different taste.

EL CONQUISTADOR MARGARITA

Makes 1 margarita

Another new import into the United States is El Conquistador. El Conquistador comes in blanco, reposado, and añejo. This margarita is made with the 100 percent agave blanco tequila. El Conquistador is packaged in a very attractive handblown blue bottle with white and gold lettering. The blanco is reasonably priced and should be available throughout the country. You're really going to enjoy the smooth taste of this margarita, as the addition of Cointreau brings out the force of the agave nose in an excellent fresh-from-the-still 100 percent agave blanco tequila.

> 1 lemon or lime wedge
> Saucer of kosher salt (about ¼ inch deep)
> 1¼ ounces El Conquistador Blanco tequila
> 1 ounce Cointreau
> 1½ ounces freshly squeezed lemon or lime juice
> Ice

Run the lemon or lime wedge around the rim of a hurricane-style margarita glass. Dip the rim of the glass into the saucer of salt, rotating the rim in the salt until the desired amount has collected on the glass.

Measure the tequila, Cointreau, and lemon or lime juice into a 16-ounce cocktail shaker glass full of ice. Place a stainless steel cocktail shaker over the glass, tapping the top to create a seal. Shake vigorously for about 5 seconds and pour into the salt-rimmed glass.

Tequila Tidbit Tequila was imported legally for the first time into the United States during the late 1800s. During the Prohibition era it was smuggled over the border from Mexico on a limited basis, but some say that because it was so easy to bring it over the border, Prohibition helped tequila to gain popularity in the United States.

Margarita Tip Maria's features a blue margarita, The Turquoise Trail, which uses blue triple sec that has been artificially colored. The strawberry margarita is red, and the peach is peach color, naturally. Why not try using food coloring in your margaritas for a special occasion— red, white, and blue for the Fourth of July, or red and green for Christmas?

TEQUILA
Conquista
BLANCO
100% DE AGAVE AZUL
HECHO EN MEXICO
Cont. Net. 750 ml

THE SOLDIER FROM SPAIN
MARGARITA

Makes 1 margarita

Conquistador *means "conqueror." Mexico was conquered, and New Mexico was settled by the conquistadors, or the soldiers of Spain. A lot of the history of tequila includes the conquistadors. It is they, for example, who decided that the pulque the Mexican Indians served them tasted so awful, they would improve the flavor by distilling it. And so tequila was born. It seems fitting that we now have a tequila named after these history makers, and even more so that we concoct a margarita that we can call "the Soldier from Spain."*

> 1 lemon or lime wedge
> Saucer of kosher salt (about ¼ inch deep)
> 1¼ ounces El Conquistador Reposado tequila
> 1 ounce Cointreau
> 1½ ounces freshly squeezed lemon or lime juice
> Ice

Run the lemon or lime wedge around the rim of a hurricane-style margarita glass. Dip the rim of the glass into the saucer of salt, rotating the rim in the salt until the desired amount has collected on the glass.

Measure the tequila, Cointreau, and lemon or lime juice into a 16-ounce cocktail shaker glass full of ice. Place a stainless steel cocktail shaker over the glass, tapping the top to create a seal. Shake vigorously for about 5 seconds and pour into the salt-rimmed glass.

Tequila Tidbit Until the Spanish conquistadors came to Mexico in the sixteenth century, the Mexican Indians had been drinking fermented juices from the blue agave plant. Commonly referred to as **pulque**, this horrible tasting nectar was offered to the conquistadors, who immediately tried to improve the flavor by distilling it. One distillation didn't improve the flavor much, so they did it a second time. Thus was born the process of making tequila—double-distilled, fermented blue agave juice.

THE BLAZING SADDLE MARGARITA

Makes 1 margarita

This margarita is basically the same as the Silver Spur Margarita (page 125) except that it uses 100 percent agave Espolon Reposado tequila instead of the Espolon Silver. Espolon means "spur," and a few months on oak has given this reposado tequila a bit of a spicy flavor. As we were tasting various concoctions to come up with a winning formula, this spicy tequila made us think of hot spurs. But being Mel Brooks fans, we went with the name "Blazing Saddle" instead.

    1 lemon or lime wedge
    Saucer of kosher salt (about ¼ inch deep)
    1¼ ounces Espolon Reposado tequila
    1 ounce Cointreau
    1½ ounces freshly squeezed lemon or lime juice
    Ice

Run the lemon or lime wedge around the rim of a hurricane-style margarita glass. Dip the rim of the glass into the saucer of salt, rotating the rim in the salt until the desired amount has collected on the glass.

Measure the tequila, Cointreau, and lemon or lime juice into a 16-ounce cocktail shaker glass full of ice. Place a stainless steel cocktail shaker over the glass, tapping the top to create a seal. Shake vigorously for about 5 seconds and pour into the salt-rimmed glass.

Margarita Tip When you serve margaritas using plastic glasses, use table salt instead of kosher salt because it sticks much better to the plastic. There's something about the coarser texture of kosher salt that just hates plastic!

Tequila Tidbit Until the 1930s, all tequila was 100 percent blue agave. Because of increasing demand, the producers began mixing in cane sugar, thus introducing the 51 percent agave tequilas that dominate the market today.

THE CASA NOBLE MARGARITA
Makes 1 margarita

You're going to pay a little bit more for this tequila because of the bottle, but you will love the contents. Mix 100 percent agave Casa Noble Añejo tequila with Cointreau, and you'll think you've died and gone to heaven. This tequila is triple distilled and aged on oak for more than the prescribed one year. Before you mix up the cocktail, pour a half ounce into a Riedel crystal tequila tasting glass and sip slowly. It's so good, you may never want to make the margarita! However, take my word for it, if you like it straight, you're going to love it in a margarita.

    1 lemon or lime wedge
    Saucer of kosher salt (about ¼ inch deep)
    1¼ ounces Casa Noble Añejo tequila
    1 ounce Cointreau
    1½ ounces freshly squeezed lemon or lime juice
    Ice

Run the lemon or lime wedge around the rim of a hurricane-style margarita glass. Dip the rim of the glass into the saucer of salt, rotating the rim in the salt until the desired amount has collected on the glass.

Measure the tequila, Cointreau, and lemon or lime juice into a 16-ounce cocktail shaker glass full of ice. Place a stainless steel cocktail shaker over the glass, tapping the top to create a seal. Shake vigorously for about 5 seconds and pour into the salt-rimmed glass.

Tequila Tidbit The ancient Mexican Indian cultures handled drunkenness (usually caused by drinking too much pulque) by shaving the perpetrator's head—the sign of disgrace—for the first offense. The punishment for a second offense was a little more harsh—death!

THE DON ALEJO MARGARITA

Makes 1 margarita

Don Alejo Blanco tequila is from Los Altos and is made by Agave Tequilana Productores, who also make Don Juan tequila. The bottle is round and the flavor is well-rounded. Mix it with Cointreau and you'll love the fresh, clean taste that this 100 percent agave silver tequila produces. Los Altos ("the highlands") of Jalisco is fast becoming a major rival to Tequila as a producer of premium-quality, 100 percent agave tequilas as its local distillers produce for more and more new importers.

    1 lemon or lime wedge
    Saucer of kosher salt (about ¼ inch deep)
    1¼ ounces Don Alejo Blanco tequila
    1 ounce Cointreau
    1½ ounces freshly squeezed lemon or lime juice
    Ice

Run the lemon or lime wedge around the rim of a hurricane-style margarita glass. Dip the rim of the glass into the saucer of salt, rotating the rim in the salt until the desired amount has collected on the glass.

Measure the tequila, Cointreau, and lemon or lime juice into a 16-ounce cocktail shaker glass full of ice. Place a stainless steel cocktail shaker over the glass, tapping the top to create a seal. Shake vigorously for about 5 seconds and pour into the salt-rimmed glass.

Tequila Tidbit Blue agave is so called because of the bluish hues that the fields of the plants give as they undulate along the hillsides of the Sierra Madre range. The juices of these plants are not, as some suppose, blue—in fact, once they have been fermented and double distilled into tequila, they are crystal clear.

THE DON EDUARDO MARGARITA
Makes 1 margarita

Don Eduardo is made by Tequila Orendain in Jalisco for Brown-Forman Beverages Worldwide Importers in Lexington, Kentucky. Don Eduardo's 100 percent agave silver tequila is different from most because it is triple distilled. The Mexican government requires that all tequilas must be at least double distilled. Don Eduardo Silver tequila is basically purified one more time, while still keeping its 80-proof (40 percent alcohol) status. For the Don Eduardo Margarita, Don Eduardo's 100 percent agave triple distilled silver tequila is mixed with triple distilled Cointreau and freshly squeezed lemon juice—how pure can you get?

> 1 lemon or lime wedge
> Saucer of kosher salt (about ¼ inch deep)
> 1¼ ounces Don Eduardo Silver tequila
> 1 ounce Cointreau
> 1½ ounces freshly squeezed lemon or lime juice
> Ice

Run the lemon or lime wedge around the rim of a hurricane-style margarita glass. Dip the rim of the glass into the saucer of salt, rotating the rim in the salt until the desired amount has collected on the glass.

Measure the tequila, Cointreau, and lemon or lime juice into a 16-ounce cocktail shaker glass full of ice. Place a stainless steel cocktail shaker over the glass, tapping the top to create a seal. Shake vigorously for about 5 seconds and pour into the salt-rimmed glass.

Tequila Tidbit When visiting Mexico, you may hear the agave plant referred to as maguey. It is still the same plant, the **Agave tequilana Weber**, blue variety. "Maguey" is what the Spanish explorers called agave when they first came into the tequila country.

THE FAT EDDIE MARGARITA
Makes 1 margarita

*This margarita is named for our old pal, Eddie Smithson, who estab-
lished the original "Fat Eddie's" in Las Cruces, New Mexico. Eddie has a
great reputation in the restaurant and hotel management business. He
was concerned that if we used an inferior tequila in a margarita sporting
his name, we would inadvertently tarnish his reputation. So, we've used
one of the very best tequilas for his namesake, 100 percent agave Don
Eduardo Añejo. Enjoy!*

> 1 lemon or lime wedge
> Saucer of kosher salt (about ¼ inch deep)
> 1¼ ounces Don Eduardo Añejo tequila
> 1 ounce Cointreau
> 1½ ounces freshly squeezed lemon or lime juice
> Ice

Run the lemon or lime wedge around the rim of a hurricane-
style margarita glass. Dip the rim of the glass into the saucer
of salt, rotating the rim in the salt until the desired amount
has collected on the glass.

Measure the tequila, Cointreau, and lemon or lime juice
into a 16-ounce cocktail shaker glass full of ice. Place a stainless steel cocktail shaker over the glass, tapping the top to
create a seal. Shake vigorously for about 5 seconds and pour
into the salt-rimmed glass.

Margarita Tip A great party idea is to organize a blind tasting
of tequilas or margaritas for your friends. Pour drinks
made with different tequilas (both silver and gold),
and compare notes. Make sure that guests arriving by
car have designated drivers—they can be put in
charge of pouring the drinks, coding them so
guests don't know ahead of time the brands
they are trying, and announcing the results.

Tequila Tidbit The word "mezcal" is
derived from the words **metl** and **valli**,
which mean "stew" or "concoction" in the
ancient Nahuatl (Aztec) language.

LA MARGARITA DE LA FIESTA

Makes 1 margarita

In old Santa Fe, the fiesta (feast day or festival) was the happiest (and most fun) day of the year. Kids were allowed to eat all the candy and junk food they wanted—and adults were allowed to eat and, more importantly, drink, what they wanted. The women of the house would make all of the old family recipes: tamales, posole, carne adovada— whatever, as long as it was special. When we first tasted 100 percent agave Don Alejo Reposado tequila mixed with Cointreau and freshly squeezed lemon juice it reminded us of an old-time celebration. Try this margarita for your next fiesta!

> 1 lemon or lime wedge
> Saucer of kosher salt (about ¼ inch deep)
> 1¼ ounces Don Alejo Reposado tequila
> 1 ounce Cointreau
> 1½ ounces freshly squeezed lemon or lime juice
> Ice

Run the lemon or lime wedge around the rim of a hurricane-style margarita glass. Dip the rim of the glass into the saucer of salt, rotating the rim in the salt until the desired amount has collected on the glass.

Measure the tequila, Cointreau, and lemon or lime juice into a 16-ounce cocktail shaker glass full of ice. Place a stainless steel cocktail shaker over the glass, tapping the top to create a seal. Shake vigorously for about 5 seconds and pour into the salt-rimmed glass.

Tequila Tidbit Once the blue agave plant has reached maturity, it must be harvested to be used for tequila production. If it is not harvested immediately upon maturity, the piña will sprout a long-stemmed flower that grows about 2 feet a day (right out of the center) and can reach a height of 6 to 12 feet. Once this occurs, the agave is no longer usable for tequila because the plant has spent its energy (in the form of the sugar) to create this incredible flower.

THE GOLDEN MIRACLE MARGARITA
Makes 1 margarita

I personally think that the Milagro line of 100 percent agave tequilas (silver, reposado, and añejo) is one of those special liquors that not only offers a high-quality, satisfying flavor, but comes in a really great bottle. I am constantly preaching against paying too much for a pretty bottle on some of the new superpremium tequilas, but in this case you may pay a little extra for the bottle, but the bottle is outstanding. The full name, Leyenda del Milagro, means the "Legend of the Miracle." This fine tequila is grown in Los Altos, "the highlands," of Jalisco. Try this recipe, then experiment with various Grand Marniers—it's fun to see which gives you the most delicious margarita.

> 1 lemon or lime wedge
> Saucer of kosher salt (about ¼ inch deep)
> 1¼ ounces Leyenda del Milagro Añejo tequila
> 1 ounce Cointreau
> 1½ ounces freshly squeezed lemon or lime juice
> Ice

Run the lemon or lime wedge around the rim of a hurricane-style margarita glass. Dip the rim of the glass into the saucer of salt, rotating the rim in the salt until the desired amount has collected on the glass.

Measure the tequila, Cointreau, and lemon or lime juice into a 16-ounce cocktail shaker glass full of ice. Place a stainless steel cocktail shaker over the glass, tapping the top to create a seal. Shake vigorously for about 5 seconds and pour into the salt-rimmed glass.

Tequila Tidbit The Aztecs used the agave plant as a food by roasting it over the fire and then eating the sweet flesh. They used the sap as a medicinal remedy, especially to heal wounds—as aloe vera is used. They also made the undistilled fermented juice into pulque, an alcoholic beverage.

THE HART TO HART MARGARITA
Makes 1 margarita

Remember the television show called Hart to Hart? It starred Robert Wagner and Stephanie Powers as the Harts, and was the first syndicated television show aired on channel two in Santa Fe, back when I was still working in television. To kick off our grand opening season in 1983, we brought Robert Wagner and his love, Jill St. John, in for a big party (Stephanie Powers was filming in South America and couldn't make it). We named a margarita after the show when we got our first shipment of Corazón ("heart") tequila. This margarita is a favorite of my wife, Laurie, and I don't know if it's because she likes the drink so much or that she still has a crush on Robert Wagner. Every time you drink this one, think about how great the late '70s and early '80s were with television fare the likes of Hart to Hart.

> 1 lemon or lime wedge
> Saucer of kosher salt (about ¼ inch deep)
> 1¼ ounces Corazón Blanco tequila
> 1 ounce Cointreau
> 1½ ounces freshly squeezed lemon or lime juice
> Ice

Run the lemon or lime wedge around the rim of a hurricane-style margarita glass. Dip the rim of the glass into the saucer of salt, rotating the rim in the salt until the desired amount has collected on the glass.

Measure the tequila, Cointreau, and lemon or lime juice into a 16-ounce cocktail shaker glass full of ice. Place a stainless steel cocktail shaker over the glass, tapping the top to create a seal. Shake vigorously for about 5 seconds and pour into the salt-rimmed glass.

Tequila Tidbit After the agave hearts have been cooked, they are left to cool for up to 36 hours to maximize the amount of natural starches that are converted to sugar. The cooked agave is then crushed to remove the sweet juice (**aguamiel**) that will become tequila. It is left to ferment in tanks, usually with the help of added yeast.

THE HEART OF GOLD MARGARITA
Makes 1 margarita

One of the difficult things we encounter by having over one hundred different margaritas at Maria's is coming up with names that tie in the nuances of the tequila on the palate, the name of the tequila, and its special attributes. When we first made this recipe using 100 percent agave Corazón Reposado tequila, we looked at the final golden product in the frosty margarita glass and said (almost in unison) "Heart of Gold!" Truly a golden delight, this tequila is one of the better imports into the United States since the turn of the century. With a flavor this good, Corazón Reposado will enhance a margarita using the prescribed amount or even a little more.

> 1 lemon or lime wedge
> Saucer of kosher salt (about ¼ inch deep)
> 1¼ ounces Corazón Reposado tequila
> 1 ounce Cointreau
> 1½ ounces freshly squeezed lemon or lime juice
> Ice

Run the lemon or lime wedge around the rim of a hurricane-style margarita glass. Dip the rim of the glass into the saucer of salt, rotating the rim in the salt until the desired amount has collected on the glass.

Measure the tequila, Cointreau, and lemon or lime juice into a 16-ounce cocktail shaker glass full of ice. Place a stainless steel cocktail shaker over the glass, tapping the top to create a seal. Shake vigorously for about 5 seconds and pour into the salt-rimmed glass.

Tequila Tidbit **Don't be confused. There are 3 types (styles) of tequila. Some distillers use different names for these types. Tequila blanco is the same as "white" or "silver," and some are even calling it "platinum." Tequila reposado is sometimes called "gold" or even "aged" (truth is, it must be aged in oak, but only for as few as 90 days). Tequila añejo is sometimes called "gold," but most generally it is simply called "añejo" or aged; it must be aged on oak for at least a year.**

THE JIMMY BUFFETT
Makes 1 margarita

Who has done more to promote the margarita than Jimmy Buffett? Well, now the folks at Seagrams have created a tequila named after Jimmy's party anthem, "Margaritaville." We mix this great silver mixto (not 100 percent agave tequila) with Bols triple sec and freshly squeezed lemon juice. Now there really is a Margaritaville! (Although we've always considered Maria's to be Margaritaville.) By the way, we also named one of our margaritas, The Margaritaville—look for it on page 112.

    1 lemon or lime wedge
    Saucer of kosher salt (about ¼ inch deep)
    1¼ ounces Margaritaville Blanco tequila
    1 ounce Bols triple sec
    1½ ounces freshly squeezed lemon or lime juice
    Ice

Run the lemon or lime wedge around the rim of a hurricane-style margarita glass. Dip the rim of the glass into the saucer of salt, rotating the rim in the salt until the desired amount has collected on the glass.

Measure the tequila, triple sec, and lemon or lime juice into a 16-ounce cocktail shaker glass full of ice. Place a stainless steel cocktail shaker over the glass, tapping the top to create a seal. Shake vigorously for about 5 seconds and pour into the salt-rimmed glass.

Tequila Tidbit The blue agave reproduces in two ways. The underground roots produce spiderlike offspring. In addition, to be on the safe side, evolution has programmed the fully mature plant to flower, set seed, and then die. The plants are harvested for tequila before this dramatic conclusion is reached.

THE LAZY LIZARD MARGARITA
Makes 1 margarita

This margarita is made with Cabo Wabo Blanco, a 100 percent agave silver tequila, and Cointreau. Van Halen frontman Sammy Hagar produces this wonderful tequila from the Tequila region of Jalisco. Sammy has a nightclub in Baja California and because of his love for tequila he contracted with Impulsora Rombo in Jalisco to make the tequila. Cabo Wabo is imported by WDL Spirits in Napa Valley. Not only is Sammy a great entertainer, he has created a great tequila that conjures peaceful images of the Baja sun, the mighty Pacific, and a lazy lizard watching it all from a warm rock.

1 lemon or lime wedge
Saucer of kosher salt (about ¼ inch deep)
1¼ ounces Cabo Wabo Blanco tequila
1 ounce Cointreau
1½ ounces freshly squeezed lemon or lime juice
Ice

Run the lemon or lime wedge around the rim of a hurricane-style margarita glass. Dip the rim of the glass into the saucer of salt, rotating the rim in the salt until the desired amount has collected on the glass.

Measure the tequila, Cointreau, and lemon or lime juice into a 16-ounce cocktail shaker glass full of ice. Place a stainless steel cocktail shaker over the glass, tapping the top to create a seal. Shake vigorously for about 5 seconds and pour into the salt-rimmed glass.

Tequila Tidbit The maximum period for aging tequila in wooden barrels is 3 to 4 years. It is one spirit that does not improve with longer aging. After 6 or 7 years in the barrel, tequila becomes unpalatable.

THE MARGARITAVILLE MARGARITA

Makes 1 margarita

Sooner or later, there had to be a tequila named for the anthem that made this wonderful cocktail a household word. Jimmy Buffett wrote it, sang it, and owns his own Margaritaville. Margaritaville tequila is made and marketed by Seagrams and is fully licensed by Señor Buffett. It is not a 100 percent agave tequila, but rest assured that it is a 100 percent high-quality mixto tequila. Way to go Jimmy!

    1 lemon or lime wedge
    Saucer of kosher salt (about ¼ inch deep)
    1¼ ounces Margaritaville Oro tequila
    1 ounce Bols triple sec
    1½ ounces freshly squeezed lemon or lime juice
    Ice

Run the lemon or lime wedge around the rim of a hurricane-style margarita glass. Dip the rim of the glass into the saucer of salt, rotating the rim in the salt until the desired amount has collected on the glass.

Measure the tequila, triple sec, and lemon or lime juice into a 16-ounce cocktail shaker glass full of ice. Place a stainless steel cocktail shaker over the glass, tapping the top to create a seal. Shake vigorously for about 5 seconds and pour into the salt-rimmed glass.

Tequila Tidbit Jimmy Buffett's song "Margaritaville" did much to spur awareness of margaritas and contribute to their popularity. The song became the unofficial anthem for the laid-back town of Key West in Florida, Jimmy Buffet's home.

THE MARK OF "Z" MARGARITA
Makes 1 margarita

During the Mexican Revolution, the revolutionaries were surrounded by enemies when a single voice let out an angry yell that motivated the men to fight with bravery to defend their ideals and freedom. This courageous battle yell was "Zafarrancho." This margarita is made with 100 percent agave Zafarrancho Reposado tequila and Cointreau, and its flavor and bouquet are far more subtle than a revolutionary battle cry.

    1 lemon or lime wedge
    Saucer of kosher salt (about ¼ inch deep)
    1¼ ounces Zafarrancho Reposado tequila
    1 ounce Cointreau
    1½ ounces freshly squeezed lemon or lime juice
    Ice

Run the lemon or lime wedge around the rim of a hurricane-style margarita glass. Dip the rim of the glass into the saucer of salt, rotating the rim in the salt until the desired amount has collected on the glass.

Measure the tequila, Cointreau, and lemon or lime juice into a 16-ounce cocktail shaker glass full of ice. Place a stainless steel cocktail shaker over the glass, tapping the top to create a seal. Shake vigorously for about 5 seconds and pour into the salt-rimmed glass.

Tequila Tidbit **Essential Spanish for the self-respecting tequilista:**
Jimador or **mescalero**—the agave field workers
Piña—the heart of the agave plant used to make tequila
Coa—the tool used to harvest the piñas

THE MERRY WIDOW MARGARITA

Makes 1 margarita

Viuda de Romero Blanco tequila is a mixto that has been around for a good period of time. Vieuda means "widow," so the name of this tequila is really "the widow of Romero" (Romero is a common surname in New Mexico). The Merry Widow Margarita was so named because it's made with a good, inexpensive mixto tequila, which means you can afford to drink several.

1 lemon or lime wedge
Saucer of kosher salt (about ¼ inch deep)
1¼ ounces Viuda de Romero Blanco tequila
1 ounce Bols triple sec
1½ ounces freshly squeezed lemon or lime juice
Ice

Run the lemon or lime wedge around the rim of a hurricane-style margarita glass. Dip the rim of the glass into the saucer of salt, rotating the rim in the salt until the desired amount has collected on the glass.

Measure the tequila, triple sec, and lemon or lime juice into a 16-ounce cocktail shaker glass full of ice. Place a stainless steel cocktail shaker over the glass, tapping the top to create a seal. Shake vigorously for about 5 seconds and pour into the salt-rimmed glass.

Tequila Tidbit All tequilas are double distilled. In the case of 100 percent agave tequila, that means simply that the fermented agave juices (**aguamiel**, literally "honey water") are distilled once, then distilled a second time into a ready-to-drink, clear, fresh product that can be bottled as a white or silver tequila immediately, or held in stainless steel tanks until the distiller is ready to bottle.

THE MILAGRO BEANFIELD MARGARITA

Makes 1 margarita

Shortly after adding the Milagro tequilas to our inventory, we sat down with Chick Vennera, one of the stars of Robert Redford's movie, The Milagro Beanfield War, *and tested various formulas for this margarita. It was easy to settle on the recipe, but as we sat there sipping this great concoction we puzzled over what to call it. We wanted to use the word* milagro *since the recipe uses 100 percent agave Milagro Reposado, but we didn't want to use the word "war." So we just ended up referring to the beanfield and the* milagro, *or "miracle," that was thought to have occurred.*

> 1 lemon or lime wedge
> Saucer of kosher salt (about ¼ inch deep)
> 1¼ ounces Leyenda del Milagro Reposado tequila
> 1 ounce Cointreau
> 1½ ounces freshly squeezed lemon or lime juice
> Ice

Run the lemon or lime wedge around the rim of a hurricane-style margarita glass. Dip the rim of the glass into the saucer of salt, rotating the rim in the salt until the desired amount has collected on the glass.

Measure the tequila, Cointreau, and lemon or lime juice into a 16-ounce cocktail shaker glass full of ice. Place a stainless steel cocktail shaker over the glass, tapping the top to create a seal. Shake vigorously for about 5 seconds and pour into the salt-rimmed glass.

Margarita Tip People tend to serve margaritas only with Mexican food. Next time you invest in a super-premium bottle of tequila, don't let it sit on a shelf until your next fiesta. Try serving about 1¼ ounces of 100 percent agave tequila in brandy snifters after dinner instead of cognac. Your guests will marvel at your good taste and sophistication.

Tequila Tidbit While there are 360 varieties of agave, blue agave is the only one from which tequila can be made. Some of the other varieties are used to make mezcal and pulque, for example.

THE PENCA AZUL LIMITED EDITION MARGARITA
Makes 1 margarita

This margarita sells for $25 on Maria's Great Margarita List. A good deal of the cost comes from the great bottle that Penca Azul comes in. The bottle was created for the Ruiz family by the award-winning maestro of mouth-blown glass in Mexico, Hipolito Gutierrez. It includes a miniature blue-glass agave plant on the bottom of the inside of the bottle. As for the tequila inside . . . Penca Azul is the masterpiece of four generations of the Ruiz family. The Hacienda "La Providencia" was the first family distillery, located in El Arenal in the state of Jalisco. They have maintained a legacy of excellence in tequila production for more than a hundred years. The Penca Azul reposado is an outstanding example of their dedication to perfection. Go ahead, try an ounce or two in a tequila tasting glass . . . but do not hesitate to pour it into a margarita using this recipe.

> 1 lemon or lime wedge
> Saucer of kosher salt (about ¼ inch deep)
> 1¼ ounces Penca Azul tequila
> 1 ounce Cointreau
> 1½ ounces freshly squeezed lemon or lime juice
> Ice

Run the lemon or lime wedge around the rim of a hurricane-style margarita glass. Dip the rim of the glass into the saucer of salt, rotating the rim in the salt until the desired amount has collected on the glass.

Measure the tequila, Cointreau, and lemon or lime juice into a 16-ounce cocktail shaker glass full of ice. Place a stainless steel cocktail shaker over the glass, tapping the top to create a seal. Shake vigorously for about 5 seconds and pour into the salt-rimmed glass.

Tequila Tidbit As you drive to Tequila from the city of Guadalajara (Mexico's second-largest city), you begin to understand why they named **Agave tequilana Weber** the "blue agave." On either side of the narrow, 2-lane asphalt highway are acre after acre of neat rows of huge agave plants. In the breeze, these noble plants create an ocean of brilliant azure as the sun highlights the blue-green color of their swordlike leaves.

THE PURASANGRE BLANCO MARGARITA
Makes 1 margarita

Purasangre 100 percent agave silver (or blanco) tequila is another new entry to the import list for premium tequilas. The name of this particular tequila means "thoroughbred." When you add "blanco" to the name, you've got a premium white (meaning it was bottled fresh from the still with no oak aging) tequila. Taste it in a Reidel tequila tasting glass before making your margarita and you'll see how good the bloodlines really are.

- 1 lemon or lime wedge
- Saucer of kosher salt (about ¼ inch deep)
- 1¼ ounces Purasangre Blanco tequila
- 1 ounce Cointreau
- 1½ ounces freshly squeezed lemon or lime juice
- Ice

Run the lemon or lime wedge around the rim of a hurricane-style margarita glass. Dip the rim of the glass into the saucer of salt, rotating the rim in the salt until the desired amount has collected on the glass.

Measure the tequila, Cointreau, and lemon or lime juice into a 16-ounce cocktail shaker glass full of ice. Place a stainless steel cocktail shaker over the glass, tapping the top to create a seal. Shake vigorously for about 5 seconds and pour into the salt-rimmed glass.

Tequila Tidbit How do the agave growers know when it's time to harvest the plants for tequila production? Reddish orange colored patches appear on the base of the leaves and the plant appears to shrink a little from its regular height as the leaf sap is drawn into the heart of the plant (the piña).

THE PURASANGRE AÑEJO MARGARITA

Makes 1 margarita

One of the purest and most authentic margaritas you can make,
100 percent agave Purasangre Añejo tequila comes from agave grown in
the highlands of Jalisco. For the price, this is one of the better tequilas.

1 lemon or lime wedge
Saucer of kosher salt (about ¼ inch deep)
1¼ ounces Purasangre Añejo tequila
1 ounce Cointreau
1½ ounces freshly squeezed lemon or lime juice
Ice

Run the lemon or lime wedge around the rim of a hurricane-style margarita glass. Dip the rim of the glass into the saucer of salt, rotating the rim in the salt until the desired amount has collected on the glass.

Measure the tequila, Cointreau, and lemon or lime juice into a 16-ounce cocktail shaker glass full of ice. Place a stainless steel cocktail shaker over the glass, tapping the top to create a seal. Shake vigorously for about 5 seconds and pour into the salt-rimmed glass.

Margarita Tip Different tequilas, as well as different combinations of triple sec, Cointreau, and Grand Marnier, are what make margaritas so flexible. The different possibilities make experimenting with margaritas so much fun.

Tequila Tidbit The word agave is a botanical term derived from the Greek for "noble"—which seems highly appropriate to us!

THE PURASANGRE REPOSADO MARGARITA

Makes 1 margarita

Like its younger sibling, Purasangre Blanco, Purasangre Reposado 100 percent agave tequila is made from agave grown in Los Altos, "the highlands," in the state of Jalisco. The town of Arandas in Los Altos is to the the highlands what the town of Tequila is to the desert or lower region of Jalisco. The word purasangre *literally means "pure blood," but the English translation is "thoroughbred." This thoroughbred tequila is 100 percent agave that has been rested on oak for at least ninety days. It comes in an unpretentious bottle and is quite reasonably priced.*

>   1 lemon or lime wedge
>   Saucer of kosher salt (about ¼ inch deep)
>   1¼ ounces Purasangre Reposado tequila
>   1 ounce Cointreau
>   1½ ounces freshly squeezed lemon or lime juice
>   Ice

Run the lemon or lime wedge around the rim of a hurricane-style margarita glass. Dip the rim of the glass into the saucer of salt, rotating the rim in the salt until the desired amount has collected on the glass.

Measure the tequila, Cointreau, and lemon or lime juice into a 16-ounce cocktail shaker glass full of ice. Place a stainless steel cocktail shaker over the glass, tapping the top to create a seal. Shake vigorously for about 5 seconds and pour into the salt-rimmed glass.

Tequila Tidbit Blue agave plants have very shallow roots—no more than 1 foot underground. The harvested plants average 40 to 80 pounds each; a few weigh as much as 200 pounds.

THE RANDALL SCANDAL MARGARITA

Makes 1 margarita

Can you handle a Randall Scandal? This margarita is named after one of Santa Fe's most colorful personalities, our hotelier friend, Randy Randall. Mr. Randall is a frequent diner at Maria's and claims that the Randall Scandal sells so well because it's named after him. It's made with a true boutique tequila: 100 percent agave Espolon Añejo tequila. Espolon means "spur," and the tequila comes in all three styles: silver, reposado, and añejo.

1 lemon or lime wedge
Saucer of kosher salt (about ¼ inch deep)
1¼ ounces Espolon Añejo tequila
1 ounce Cointreau
1½ ounces freshly squeezed lemon or lime juice
Ice

Run the lemon or lime wedge around the rim of a hurricane-style margarita glass. Dip the rim of the glass into the saucer of salt, rotating the rim in the salt until the desired amount has collected on the glass.

Measure the tequila, Cointreau, and lemon or lime juice into a 16-ounce cocktail shaker glass full of ice. Place a stainless steel cocktail shaker over the glass, tapping the top to create a seal. Shake vigorously for about 5 seconds and pour into the salt-rimmed glass.

Margarita Tip It's no wonder that margaritas are associated with good times and wonderful memories—it's a tradition. A passage from a book called **Tequila, lo Nuestro** (published by Sauza) reads in translation: "In every drop of tequila, of our tequila, there is a spirit of the hospitality of our land and the promise of a fiesta. Of a fiesta that never ends. The fiesta of the tequila." Well, since the key ingredient in a margarita is tequila, it stands to reason that good times can be expected from drinking them.

LA MARGARITA DEL EL RATON MICKEY

Makes 1 margarita

There is no word for "mouse" in Spanish; consequently, we had to name our Mouse Margarita the El Raton Mickey, or "Mickey the Rat." The real force behind the name is Mickey Cerletti, who has been the secretary of tourism for the state of New Mexico and the manager of Expo-New Mexico, the New Mexico State Fair. Mickey is a good friend and has helped us name more than one margarita in the past. We use 100 percent agave Zafarrancho Blanco/Silver tequila and Cointreau. Not only is this a great tequila, you're going to love the bottle.

> 1 lemon or lime wedge
> Saucer of kosher salt (about ¼ inch deep)
> 1¼ ounces Zafarrancho Blanco/Silver tequila
> 1 ounce Cointreau
> 1½ ounces freshly squeezed lemon or lime juice
> Ice

Run the lemon or lime wedge around the rim of a hurricane-style margarita glass. Dip the rim of the glass into the saucer of salt, rotating the rim in the salt until the desired amount has collected on the glass.

Measure the tequila, Cointreau, and lemon or lime juice into a 16-ounce cocktail shaker glass full of ice. Place a stainless steel cocktail shaker over the glass, tapping the top to create a seal. Shake vigorously for about 5 seconds and pour into the salt-rimmed glass.

Margarita Tip Try to serve your margaritas in stemware. For its "rocks" glass, Maria's uses a hurricane-style glass made by Libbey, called the "Poco Grande." The "up" glass we use is also from Libbey and is called the "Coupette." If your favorite kitchen- or bar-supply store does not stock them, ask them to order by name from Libbey.

121

THE SILVER CHARM MARGARITA
Makes 1 margarita

Milagro (which means "miracle") 100 percent agave tequila is a relatively new entry into the United States. It's no miracle that we were quick to add this product to our inventory and tequila list. The Silver Charm Margarita is one of the smoothest margaritas on our list. It has a certain charm about it.

> 1 lemon or lime wedge
> Saucer of kosher salt (about ¼ inch deep)
> 1¼ ounces Leyenda del Milagro Silver tequila
> 1 ounce Cointreau
> 1½ ounces freshly squeezed lemon or lime juice
> Ice

Run the lemon or lime wedge around the rim of a hurricane-style margarita glass. Dip the rim of the glass into the saucer of salt, rotating the rim in the salt until the desired amount has collected on the glass.

Measure the tequila, Cointreau, and lemon or lime juice into a 16-ounce cocktail shaker glass full of ice. Place a stainless steel cocktail shaker over the glass, tapping the top to create a seal. Shake vigorously for about 5 seconds and pour into the salt-rimmed glass.

Tequila Tidbit If you ever plan a trip to see the tequila distilleries, an indispensable guide is **The Tequila Lover's Guide to Mexico**, written by Lance Cutler and published by the Wine Patrol Press in 1998. Cutler, a California winemaker, taste tests tequilas and offers a very helpful travel guide.

THE SILVER SPUR MARGARITA
Makes 1 margarita

For this margarita we use a 100 percent agave silver tequila made by Epsolon (which means "spurs"). Every once in a while, with Santa Fe being Santa Fe, someone will walk into the restaurant wearing spurs. Generally, if he's a working cowboy, his spurs will be made of steel or some other nonprecious metal. If that cowboy is planning to be in a parade or performing in a band, those spurs just might be made of silver. In the days of the Spanish grandees, silver spurs were a sign of wealth.

> 1 lemon or lime wedge
> Saucer of kosher salt (about ¼ inch deep)
> 1¼ ounces Espolon Silver tequila
> 1 ounce Cointreau
> 1½ ounces freshly squeezed lemon or lime juice
> Ice

Run the lemon or lime wedge around the rim of a hurricane-style margarita glass. Dip the rim of the glass into the saucer of salt, rotating the rim in the salt until the desired amount has collected on the glass.

Measure the tequila, Cointreau, and lemon or lime juice into a 16-ounce cocktail shaker glass full of ice. Place a stainless steel cocktail shaker over the glass, tapping the top to create a seal. Shake vigorously for about 5 seconds and pour into the salt-rimmed glass.

Margarita Tip In addition to Realemon as a substitute for fresh lemon or lime juice, Minute Maid produces a frozen nonconcentrated pure lemon juice that has no additives. Under no circumstances should you use a sweetened lemon or lime juice such as frozen lemonade or frozen limeade. With the added sugar in these products, you'll end up with an icky-sweet margarita that's a waste of good tequila.

Tequila Tidbit Tequila does not share quite the long history of pulque or mezcal; it dates from the late seventeenth century, but production only began in earnest in the last quarter of the nineteenth century.

LA MARGARITA DE LA VIUDA DE ROMERO
Makes 1 margarita

Viuda de Romero is one of the older tequila houses in Jalisco. Their tequila has only recently been imported into the United States and shows how good a quality mixto tequila can be. This is made with their reposado and one of the few mixtos that is of a quality good enough to be aged on oak. It's a very affordable tequila and makes a wonderful margarita.

1 lemon or lime wedge
Saucer of kosher salt (about ¼ inch deep)
1¼ ounces Viuda de Romero Reposado tequila
1 ounce Bols triple sec
1½ ounces freshly squeezed lemon or lime juice
Ice

Run the lemon or lime wedge around the rim of a hurricane-style margarita glass. Dip the rim of the glass into the saucer of salt, rotating the rim in the salt until the desired amount has collected on the glass.

Measure the tequila, triple sec, and lemon or lime juice into a 16-ounce cocktail shaker glass full of ice. Place a stainless steel cocktail shaker over the glass, tapping the top to create a seal. Shake vigorously for about 5 seconds and pour into the salt-rimmed glass.

Margarita Tip Take particular care in washing your margarita shakers and glasses if you're using freshly squeezed juices. The pulp has a tendency to adhere to the surface of the utensil. Your best bet is to rinse the shaker and glasses as soon as possible after drinking the margarita, before the pulp has a chance to dry on the surface.

THE USS *SANTA FE* FAST-ATTACK MARGARITA

Makes 1 margarita

With this margarita we salute the USS Santa Fe *fast-attack nuclear submarine and its outstanding crew. The city of Santa Fe's namesake is stationed in Honolulu, but the commanding officer and crew make it a point to visit our city and enjoy the margaritas and food at Maria's. This margarita is special because of the people we salute with its name. We use 100 percent agave Don Alvaro Silver tequila with Cointreau and freshly squeezed lemon juice for a "smooth as a ride in a nuclear submarine" cocktail.*

> 1 lemon or lime wedge
> Saucer of kosher salt (about ¼ inch deep)
> 1¼ ounces Don Alvaro Silver tequila
> 1 ounce Cointreau
> 1½ ounces freshly squeezed lemon or lime juice
> Ice

Run the lemon or lime wedge around the rim of a hurricane-style margarita glass. Dip the rim of the glass into the saucer of salt, rotating the rim in the salt until the desired amount has collected on the glass.

Measure the tequila, Cointreau, and lemon or lime juice into a 16-ounce cocktail shaker glass full of ice. Place a stainless steel cocktail shaker over the glass, tapping the top to create a seal. Shake vigorously for about 5 seconds and pour into the salt-rimmed glass.

Margarita Tip If a guest complains that the margarita masterpiece you just made and served is too tart, simply add a little triple sec, Cointreau, or Grand Marnier to sweeten it up. Never add sugar. If this happens, cut back on the lemon or lime juice, and add a little water to the juice for dilution.

129

THE MANGO MARGARITA
Makes 1 cocktail

We were at the José Cuervo Hacienda in Tequila, Jalisco, several years ago and had one of their mango margaritas. It was really good—a little sweet, but refreshing and delicious. I asked the bartender if they were using fresh mangoes, but he showed me a can of mangoes packed in syrup. We try to avoid adding extra sugar to our margaritas, so when we returned to Santa Fe we asked a supplier if they had canned or frozen unsweetened mango. Our sales rep informed us that they had only recently added individually quick-frozen mangoes with no sugar added to their inventory. Wow, what a treat! If you want to substitute for unsweetened quick-frozen mangoes, use very ripe fresh or frozen unsweetened mangoes. If unsweetened mangoes aren't sweet enough, you can add simple syrup or sweet-and-sour mix to taste. (Heck, even if you use sweetened mangoes, you're going to love this cocktail!)

- 1¼ ounces José Cuervo Especial tequila
- 1 ounce Bols triple sec
- 1½ ounces freshly squeezed lemon or lime juice
- ¼ to ⅓ cup frozen, thawed, or fresh mango chunks
- 2 ounces simple syrup (see page 131) or sweet-and-sour mix (optional)
- 2 cups cracked ice

Place all of the ingredients in a blender and blend until smooth. Pour the mixture into a hurricane-style margarita glass.

THE PEACH MARGARITA

Makes 1 cocktail

Use the ripest, juiciest peaches you can find and slice them over the blender so you don't waste a drop of the nectar. As with the preceding recipe, use unsweetened individually frozen peaches if the fresh fruit is out of season, but avoid sweetened frozen peaches as the drink will be too sweet. Be careful—these fruit cocktails are so delicious and flavorful that you tend to forget they contain alcohol.

- 1¼ ounces José Cuervo Gold tequila
- 1 ounce Bols triple sec
- 1½ ounces freshly squeezed lemon juice
- 2 ounces simple syrup (see page 131) or sweet-and-sour mix
- 1 peeled, pitted, and sliced fresh peach, or ¾ cup partially frozen peach slices
- 2 cups cracked ice

Place all of the ingredients in a blender and blend until smooth. Pour the mixture into a hurricane-style margarita glass.

THE CHIMAYO COCKTAIL

Makes 1 cocktail

Chimayo is an old village in a valley of the Sangre de Cristo mountains that was originally settled by the Spanish in the seventeenth century. It's located about thirty miles north of Santa Fe and remains a charming place that's well-known for the healing properties of the holy dirt in the santuario (or church). Chimayo is also famous for its outstanding New Mexico red chiles, probably the best chiles in the world, as well as for its delicious red apples. The Jaramillo family invented this cocktail to promote the village and its apples, many of which are harvested in the orchards around its famous restaurant—the picturesque Rancho de Chimayó.

- Ice
- 1¼ ounces Herradura Silver tequila
- ¼ ounce crème de cassis
- 1 ounce fresh apple cider or juice
- ¼ ounce freshly squeezed lemon juice
- 1 red apple wedge

Fill a double old-fashioned glass with ice. Pour the tequila, crème de cassis, apple cider or juice, and lemon juice over the ice, and stir. Garnish the glass with an apple wedge and serve.

TEQUILA SUNRISE

Makes 1 cocktail

After the margarita, the Tequila Sunrise is perhaps the oldest and most popular tequila drink. As with all of these recipes, the better the ingredients, the better the final product. Use freshly squeezed juice and a good tequila; if ordering this at a bar or restaurant, be sure to avoid the house "well" brand, unless you know it's a premium tequila like Cuervo or Sauza (Cuervo Gold is the "well" tequila at Maria's).

- Ice
- 6 ounces freshly squeezed orange juice
- 1¼ ounces José Cuervo Gold tequila
- Splash of grenadine
- 1 orange or lime wedge, or 1 maraschino cherry on a toothpick, for garnish (optional)

Fill a double old-fashioned glass three-quarters full of ice. Add the orange juice and tequila and stir. Add the grenadine. Garnish the glass with a fruit wedge or cherry, and serve.

THE LUCERO DE LA MAÑANA

Makes 1 cocktail

This is one of the most refreshing eye-openers you could imagine. The name of the cocktail is a pun on its creator's name (your humble author) and the translation is "morning star." It'll certainly be the star of your next breakfast or brunch party. Remember: the fresher and colder the orange juice, the better the drink.

- Ice
- 1¼ ounces El Tesoro Platinum tequila
- 8 ounces freshly squeezed orange juice
- Splash of cranberry juice
- 1 orange or lime slice for garnish (optional)

Fill a 16-ounce tumbler with ice. Pour the tequila over the ice. Add the orange juice and stir. Add the cranberry juice and serve. Garnish with an orange or lime slice.

NEW MEXICO FAMILY-STYLE TACOS

Serves 6 (makes 12 tacos)

This simple recipe can be halved, doubled, tripled, or whatever. The recipe was designed for soft tacos (with the tortillas kept warm by covering them with a cloth), but the crisp U-shaped taco shells are a treat, as well. You can add a bowl of sour cream, guacamole, or different taco sauces or salsas according to your fancy.

> 1 pound extra-lean ground beef
> Vegetable oil for frying
> 12 yellow or blue corn tortillas
> 1 yellow onion, coarsely chopped
> 2 ripe tomatoes, coarsely chopped
> 2 cups (8 ounces) shredded Cheddar cheese
> 1/2 head iceberg lettuce, coarsely chopped
> Maria's World-Famous Salsa (see page 141) or your
>   favorite taco sauce or salsa
> Salt and pepper to taste

In a large skillet or sauté pan, sauté the ground beef until cooked through and browned. Drain off the fat and place the beef in a large serving bowl.

In another skillet or sauté pan, heat about 1/2 inch of vegetable oil until very hot. Fry a tortilla for 5 to 10 seconds, or just until softened, holding it with cooking tongs. Do not allow the tortilla to become crisp.

Place the tortilla on a paper towel on a serving plate and repeat until all the tortillas are fried, layering paper towels between them to absorb the oil. If not serving immediately, cover the tortillas with a clean dish towel to keep warm.

Place the onion, tomatoes, cheese, lettuce, and salsa in separate serving bowls in the center of the table along with the meat and tortillas. Place a tortilla on a serving plate, spoon some beef in the center of the tortilla, add salsa or taco sauce, salt, and pepper, then sprinkle a little onion, tomato, cheese, and lettuce on top of the beef (in that order). Fold the tortilla to form a soft taco, pick it up, and eat.

MARIA'S BLUE CORN ENCHILADAS

Makes 4 servings

Grind your own dried New Mexico red chiles or use pure New Mexico red chile powder for this recipe. Any other chile powder is just not the same. To make a vegetarian chile sauce, just eliminate the ground beef.

Red Chile Enchilada Sauce

- 2 tablespoons vegetable shortening or lard
- 9 heaping tablespoons New Mexico red chile powder
- 4 quarts cold water
- 1 heaping tablespoon all-purpose flour
- 4 cloves garlic, minced
- 1 teaspoon salt
- 2 pounds extra-lean ground beef

Enchiladas

- Vegetable oil for frying
- 12 blue, yellow, or white corn tortillas
- 2 cups coarsely chopped onions
- 2 cups coarsely chopped tomatoes
- 4 cups (1 pound) shredded Cheddar cheese
- 1/2 head iceberg lettuce, shredded

To prepare the enchilada sauce, melt the shortening or lard in a large saucepan over medium-high heat until just smoking. Add the chile powder, 1 tablespoon at a time, whisking constantly to avoid lumping. When too thick to whisk, add 1/2 cup of the water. Heat a little and continue to add the chile powder, alternating with the water, until all the water and all the chile powder have been combined.

In a small bowl, mix the flour with a little water until the flour is dissolved. Add this mixture to the chile powder mixture and bring to a light boil. Stir in the garlic and salt. Set aside and keep warm.

Sauté the ground beef in a large skillet or sauté pan until medium-rare. Drain off the fat and add the ground beef to the enchilada sauce. Cook for 45 minutes to 1 hour, stirring occasionally.

Preheat the oven to 200°F.

To prepare the enchiladas, heat about 1/2 inch of vegetable oil in a medium skillet until very hot. Fry one tortilla at a time for 5 to 10 seconds, or just until softened. Do not allow the tortillas to become crisp. Drain the excess oil by holding the tortillas with tongs over the pan.

Drop one tortilla into the enchilada sauce to saturate, then place it flat on a deep individual ovenproof plate or dish. Sprinkle some of the onions, tomatoes, and cheese over the tortilla, and top with an additional ¼ cup of the enchilada sauce. Saturate a second tortilla in Red Chile Enchilada Sauce and place it over the first. Top with onions, tomatoes, and cheese and another ¼ cup of the enchilada sauce.

Top with a third tortilla (the tortillas will look like a stack of pancakes covered with red chile sauce). Spoon enchilada sauce over the top of the stack and sprinkle with cheese.

Place the tortilla stack in the preheated oven. Repeat the process for 3 more serving plates or dishes. Serve at once, garnished with the lettuce and remaining chopped tomatoes, and accompanied with your favorite margarita.

MARIA'S WORLD-FAMOUS SALSA
Makes about 3 cups

This is a great taco sauce for the recipe on page 139, and it is ideal as a dip with corn tortilla chips.

> 2 cups chunky tomato sauce
> 1 cup seeded and chopped New Mexico green chiles
> ½ cup water
> ½ teaspoon salt
> 1 tablespoon minced garlic
> ¼ cup diced yellow onion
> 2 tablespoons crushed red chile flakes or chile powder

Combine all the ingredients well in a mixing bowl and adjust seasonings to taste. Cover and chill. Keep refrigerated for up to 3 days.

MARIA'S FRIJOLES

Makes about 8 cups

This bean recipe is so easy, so inexpensive, and so delicious that it should become a staple in anyone's repertoire of Southwestern food. It's also the perfect base for refried beans (see below). Use only pinto beans for this recipe, and ask for "new crop" if you have a choice. Never leave a pot of beans to cook while you leave the house; they could go dry and burn (it's happened).

> 1 pound dried pinto beans
> 4 quarts water
> 6 ounces salt pork, cut into ½-inch cubes

Thoroughly sort through the beans to remove any foreign objects such as stones or twigs. Rinse the beans under cold water and place in a large (at least 8-quart) stew pot covered with the water. Soak for 1 to 2 hours, or overnight.

Add the salt pork to the beans and soaking water and bring to a rolling boil. Reduce the heat and simmer, uncovered, for at least 2 hours, or until tender enough to mash. Add more water if at any time the beans are covered by less than 2 inches. Stir from time to time to make sure the beans are not sticking to the bottom of the pot. The longer the beans cook, the better they will taste.

For Vegetarian Frijoles Replace the salt pork with 2 tablespoons of vegetable shortening and add salt during the last 30 minutes of cooking (adding salt earlier will make the beans tough).

For Refried Beans Mash the drained, cooked beans with a fork and simmer in hot bacon fat or vegetable oil for about 10 minutes, stirring constantly.

AL'S CHEDDAR CHEESE AND ONION BEAN DIP

Makes about 8 cups

Here's a great bean dip that uses ingredients that are available just about anywhere. It's easy to make and virtually foolproof, but it does require some time and effort to prepare, as well as a chafing dish, fondue dish, or some kind of heated serving apparatus to keep the dip warm (a crockpot at its lowest setting would also work). You can make a smaller amount of the dip by dividing the recipe in half.

- 1 tablespoon solid vegetable shortening
- 4 cups drained Maria's Frijoles, broth reserved (page 142)
- 1 large onion, diced
- 3 cloves garlic, finely minced
- 1 cup Maria's World-Famous Salsa (page 141) or other picante tomato-based salsa
- 1 cup seeded and chopped New Mexico green chiles
- 4 cups (1 pound) shredded Cheddar cheese
- Tortilla chips

In a large skillet or sauté pan, melt the shortening over medium-high heat. Add the beans and mash them while frying. Lower the heat and continue to fry the mashed beans until heated through.

Transfer the beans to a large saucepan, adding the onion, garlic, salsa, and green chiles. Cook over medium heat, stirring constantly. Slowly add the cheese, stirring to blend (if the mixture becomes too thick, add a little of the reserved bean broth). Once the mixture is blended smoothly, transfer to a chafing dish, fondue dish, or crockpot. Serve with tortilla chips.

INDEX

Absolut Margarita, 136
Agave plant
    Aztec use of, 105
    botany of, 6, 115, 118, 119
    color of, 116
    growing, 61
    harvesting, 110, 117
    leaves of, 61
    liquors from, 8, 48, 77, 91, 123
    name of, 116, 118
    size of, 127
    Spanish terms regarding, 113
    sugar from, 4, 6–7, 127
Al's Cheddar Cheese and Onion Bean
    Dip, 143
Aztecs, 37, 48, 82, 103, 105

Baile del Sol Margarita, 68
Blazing Saddle Margarita, 99
Bloody Maria, 135
Boogie Woogie, 95
Buffett, Jimmy, 8, 32, 36, 110
Brass Monkey Margarita, 77

Cabo Wabo tequila, 88, 90, 111
    Hagar's Revenge Margarita, 90
    Lazy Lizard Margarita, 111
    Margarita El Cabo Wabo Kevin, 88
Casa Noble tequila, 100, 107, 127
    Casa Noble Margarita, 100
    Grand Noble Margarita, 107
    Three Nobles Margarita, 127
Casta tequila, 86
Cazadores tequila, 91
Chamucos tequila, 95
Chimayó Cocktail, 133
Chinaco tequila, 10, 11, 49–54, 68
    Baile del Sol Margarita, 68
    Chinaco Clásico Margarita, 52
    Chinaco Añejo Margarita, 53
    Gran Chinaco Margarita, 54
    Margarita del Chinaco Blanco, 50
    Margarita del Chinaco Puro, 51
Cointreau, 14–15
    Absolut Margarita, 136
    Baile del Sol Margarita, 68
    Blazing Saddle Margarita, 99
    Boogie Woogie, 95
    Casa Noble Margarita, 100
    Chinaco Añejo Margarita, 53
    Conquistador Margarita, 97
    Dandy Randy Randy, 89
    Don Alejo Margarita, 101
    Don Eduardo Margarita, 102
    Don Julio de Oro Margarita, 80
    Don Julio Plata Margarita, 82
    Don Roberto Margarita, 73
    1800 Masterpiece Margarita, 40
    1812 Overture Margarita, 37
    Elizabeth II Margarita, 63
    Fat Eddie Margarita, 103
    Golden Miracle Margarita, 105
    Goldhamer Margarita, 83
    Gran Centenario Margarita, 85

Grand Noble Margarita, 107
Gusano Margarita, 86
Hacienda Corralejo Margarita, 96
Hagar's Revenge Margarita, 90
Hart to Hart Margarita, 108
Heart of Gold Margarita, 109
Herradura Añejo Margarita, 60
Herradura Fuerte Margarita, 57
Herradura Gold Margarita, 59
Horny Toad Margarita, 46
Hussong's Special Margarita, 92
José Cuervo Tradicional Margarita, 39
Lazy Lizard Margarita, 111
Margarita Cazadores, 91
Margarita de la Doña Helen, 74
Margarita de la Patróna, 76
Margarita del Chinaco Blanco, 50
Margarita del Chinaco Puro, 51
Margarita del Dueño, 94
Margarita del El Raton Mickey, 121
Margarita del Joven Esteban, 70
Margarita de los Dos Angeles, 93
Margarita El Cabo Wabo Kevin, 88
Margarita El Jimador, 87
Maria's Famous La Ultima Margarita, 64
Mark of "Z" Margarita, 113
Mejor de Sauza, 48
Milagro Beanfield Margarita, 115
Moonglow Margarita, 66
Penca Azul Limited Edition
    Margarita, 116
Purasangre Añejo, Margarita, 118
Purasangre Blanco Margarita, 117
Purasangre Reposado Margarita, 119
Rafael Margarita, 36
Randall Scandal Margarita, 120
Santiago Margarita, 58
Sauza Conmemorativo Margarita, 47
Silver Charm Margarita, 124
Silver Spur Margarita, 125
Smooth Sioux Margarita, 126
Soldier from Spain Margarita, 96
Sue "Gee!" Margarita, 61
Three G's Margarita, 45
Three Nobles Margarita, 127
USS Santa Fe Fast-Attack Margarita, 129
Corazón tequila, 108–109
    Hart to Hart Margarita, 108
    Heart of Gold Margarita, 109
Corralejo tequila, 89, 96
    Dandy Randy Randy, 89
    Hacienda Corralejo Margarita, 96
Crowley, Martin, 10
Cuervo tequila, 31–41, 131–134
    Bloody Maria, 135
    Cuervo Clásico Margarita, 34
    1800 Masterpiece Margarita, 40
    1812 Overture Margarita, 37
    Grand Gold Margarita, 38
    José Cuervo Tradicional Margarita, 39
    Mango Margarita, 132
    Maria's 100 Percent Agave House
        Margarita, 33
    Maria's Special Margarita, 32

Peach Margarita, 133
Rafael Margarita, 36
Strawberry Margarita, 131
Tequila Sunrise, 134
Turquoise Trail Margarita, 35
24-Karat Gold Reserva Margarita, 41
Curaçao, blue, 26, 35, 88

Dandy Randy Randy, 89
Denton, Bob, 10–11, 49
Don Alejo tequila, 101, 104
Don Alejo Margarita, 101
Margarita de la Fiesta, 104
Don Alvaro tequila, 106, 126, 129
Margarita de El Gran Viejito Alvaro, 106
Smooth Sioux Margarita, 126
USS Santa Fe Fast-Attack Margarita, 129
Don Eduardo tequila, 102–3
Don Eduardo Margarita, 102
Fat Eddie Margarita, 103
Don Julio tequila, 79–83
Don Julio de Oro Margarita, 80
Don Julio Plata Margarita, 82
Goldhamer Margarita, 83
Gran Julio Reserva Margarita, 81
Don Roberto Margarita, 73

1800 Masterpiece Margarita, 40
1812 Overture Margarita, 37
El Conquistador tequila, 97–98
El Conquistador Margarita, 97
Soldier from Spain Margarita, 98
Elizabeth II Margarita, 63
El Jimador tequila, 87, 93
Margarita de los Dos Angeles, 93
Margarita El Jimador, 87
El Tesoro tequila, 10, 62–71, 134–135
Baile del Sol Margarita, 68
Elizabeth II Margarita, 63
Grand Moonglow Margarita, 67
Grand Platinum Margarita, 65
Grand Treasure Margarita, 69
Gulf Breeze, 135
Lucero de la Mañana, 134
Margarita del Joven Esteban, 70
Margarita de Paradiso, 71
Maria's Famous La Ultima Margarita, 64
Moonglow Margarita, 66
Enchiladas, 140–41
Espolon tequila, 99, 120
Blazing Saddle Margarita, 99
Randall Scandal Margarita, 120
Silver Spur Margarita, 125

Fat Eddie Margarita, 103
Felton, Larry, 75
Frijoles, 142

Gaspar, José, 25
Golden Miracle Margarita, 105
Goldhamer Margarita, 83
Gran Centenario tequila, 85
Gran Chinaco Margarita, 54
Gran Julio Reserva Margarita, 81
Grand Gold Margarita, 38

Grand Lorenzo Margarita, 75
Grand Marnier, 14–15, 36, 41, 66, 71, 88, 89, 91, 118, 129
Chinaco Clásico Margarita, 52
Elizabeth II Margarita, 63
Gran Chinaco Margarita, 54
Grand Gold Margarita, 38
Grand Lorenzo Margarita, 75
Grand Moonglow Margarita, 67
Grand Platinum Margarita, 65
Grand Treasure Margarita, 69
Gran Julio Reserva Margarita, 81
Margarita de Paradiso, 71
Smooth Sioux Margarita, 126
24-Karat Gold Reserva Margarita, 41
Grand Moonglow Margarita, 67
Grand Noble Margarita, 107
Grand Platinum Margarita, 65
Grand Treasure Margarita, 69
Guacamole, 138
Gulf Breeze, 135
Gusano Margarita, 86

Hacienda Corralejo Margarita, 96
Hacienda del Cristero Blanco tequila, 61
Hagar, Sammy, 88, 90, 111
Hagar's Revenge Margarita, 90
Hart to Hart Margarita, 108
Heart of Gold Margarita, 109
Herradura tequila, 55–61, 133
Chimayó Cocktail, 133
Herradura Añejo Margarita, 60
Herradura Fuerte Margarita, 57
Herradura Gold Margarita, 59
Santiago Margarita, 58
Silver Herradura Margarita, 56
Sue "Gee!" Margarita, 61
Herrera, Carlos, 21, 23, 27
Hinton, Red, 24
Horny Toad Margarita, 46
Hussong's tequila, 92

Jimmy Buffett, 110
José Cuervo tequila. See Cuervo tequila

King, Marjorie, 23, 27

Lazy Lizard Margarita, 111
Leyenda del Milagro tequila, 105, 115, 124
Golden Miracle Margarita, 105
Milagro Beanfield Margarita, 115
Silver Charm Margarita, 124
Lucero de la Mañana, 134

Mango Margarita, 132
Margarita Cazadores, 91
Margarita de El Gran Viejito Alvaro, 106
Margarita de la Doña Helen, 74
Margarita de la Fiesta, 104
Margarita de la Patróna, 76
Margarita de la Viuda de Romero, 128
Margarita de los Dos Angeles, 93
Margarita de Paradiso, 71
Margarita del Chinaco Blanco, 50
Margarita del Chinaco Puro, 51
Margarita del Dueño, 94

Margarita del El Raton Mickey, 121
Margarita del Joven Esteban, 70
Margarita El Cabo Wabo Kevin, 88
Margarita El Jimador, 87
Margarita Serafina Reposado, 123
Margaritas. See also individual recipes
    alcohol content of, 6, 106
    blended, 3, 14, 24
    commercial mixes for, 15, 30
    food coloring in, 35, 97
    froth on, 51
    origin of, 20–27
    storing, 87
    taste test, 30, 124
Margaritaville tequila, 110, 112
    Jimmy Buffett, 110
    Margaritaville Margarita, 112
Maria's Blue Corn Enchiladas, 140–41
Maria's Famous La Ultima Margarita, 64
Maria's Frijoles, 142
Maria's 100 Percent Agave House
    Margarita, 33
Maria's Special Margarita, 32
Maria's World-Famous Salsa, 141
Mark of "Z" Margarita, 113
Mejor de Sauza, 48
Merry Widow Margarita, 114
Mezcal, 34, 77, 86, 90, 103, 113, 123, 125
Mico de Plata Margarita, 78
Milagro Beanfield Margarita, 115
Moonglow Margarita, 66
Morales, Francisco "Pancho," 25–26

Negrete, Danny, 24
New Mexico Family-Style Tacos, 139
NOM numbers, 31, 40, 78

Patrón tequila, 11, 72–78
    Brass Monkey Margarita, 77
    Don Roberto Margarita, 73
    Grand Lorenzo Margarita, 75
    Margarita de la Doña Helen, 74
    Margarita de la Patróna, 76
    Mico de Plata Margarita, 78
Peach Margarita, 133
Penca Azul tequila, 116
Platinum Pyramid, 94
Ponce de Leon, Juan, 25
Pulque, 48, 96, 98, 100, 105, 115, 125
Purasangre tequila, 117–119

Rafael Margarita, 36
Rancho La Gloria, 21
Randall Scandal Margarita, 120
Red Chile Enchilada Sauce, 140
Reserva del Dueño tequila, 94

Sames, Margarita, 21
San Matias tequila, 122
Santiago Margarita, 58
Sauza tequila, 42–48
    Horny Toad Margarita, 46
    Mejor de Sauza, 48
    Sauza Conmemorativo Margarita, 47
    Sauza Gold Margarita, 44
    Sauza Silver Margarita, 43
    Three G's Margarita, 45

Serafina tequila, 123
Silver Charm Margarita, 124
Silver Herradura Margarita, 56
Silver Spur Margarita, 125
Smith, Marilyn, 10
Smooth Sioux Margarita, 126
Soldier from Spain Margarita, 98
Strawberry Margarita, 131
Sue "Gee!" Margarita, 61

Tail o' the Cock, 21, 26–27
Tequila, See also individual manufacturers
    agave maturity and, 106
    agave sugar in, 6–7, 50, 84
    aging, 8, 44, 45, 46, 50, 59, 60, 69, 92, 111
    as an after-dinner drink, 35, 69, 115
    best-selling, 6, 31, 76
    consumption of, 76
    double distilled, 6, 27, 63, 69, 74, 101
    expensive, 31, 127
    history of, 10–11, 98, 125
    Nahuatl, meaning of, 37, 82, 103
    NOM numbers, 31, 40, 78
    premium vs. superpremium, 7, 9,
    proof level of, 47
    regulations regarding, 6, 50, 77
    songs about, 36
    worms and, 9, 86
Tequila, Mexico, 37, 42, 66, 82, 116
Tequila Producers Association, 122
Tequila Sunrise, 134
Three G's Margarita, 45
Three Nobles Margarita, 127
Triple sec, 3, 6, 14, 21, 23–4, 36, 47, 56, 66,
    73, 89, 91, 97, 98, 118, 129
    Brass Monkey Margarita, 77
    Cuervo Clásico Margarita, 34
    Jimmy Buffett, 110
    Mango Margarita, 132
    Margarita de la Viuda de Romero, 128
    Margarita Serafina Reposado, 123
    Margaritaville Margarita, 112
    Maria's 100 Percent Agave House
        Margarita, 33
    Maria's Special Margarita, 32
    Merry Widow Margarita, 114
    Mico de Plata Margarita, 78
    Peach Margarita, 133
    San Matias Fault Margarita, 122
    Sauza Gold Margarita, 44
    Sauza Silver Margarita, 43
    Silver Herradura Margarita, 56
    Strawberry Margarita, 131
    Turquoise Trail Margarita, 35
    24-Karat Gold Reserva Margarita, 41

Underwood, Vernon, 26–27
USS Santa Fe Fast-Attack Margarita, 129

Viuda de Romero tequila, 114
    Margarita de la Viuda de Romero, 128
    Merry Widow Margarita, 114
Vodka, 136

Zafarrancho tequila, 113, 121
    Margarita del El Raton Mickey, 121
    Mark of "Z" Margarita, 113